Praise for Breaking Free

"Noer has written a book that will have profound impact, focusing people's attention on the new reality and moving them toward action."
>—JOHN D. MCCLURE, deputy minister, Department of Western Economic
>Diversification, Government of Canada

"If you are working at any level in an organization that is under stress—and who isn't these days—you should devour this book, and keep it handy!"
>—WALTER F. ULMER, JR., Lt. General U.S. Army (retired), former
>Commandant of Cadets, U.S. Military Academy, West Point, and
>president (retired), Center for Creative Leadership

"David Noer has hit the bull's-eye. *Breaking Free* is a lively and penetrating look at the real power of empowerment, full of wisdom and yet utterly practical. A very refreshing and compelling read—highly recommended!"
>—RICHARD J. LEIDER, founder and partner, The Inventure Group, and author
>of *Repacking Your Bags* and *The Power of Purpose*

"Let's face it—the old way of corporate life is gone. As David Noer so candidly notes, nowadays 'we are all temps.' This book provides a new way of looking at the world of work. The strategies offered in *Breaking Free* can help us be true to ourselves, serve others, and ultimately be more productive members of our organizations."
>—MARSHALL GOLDSMITH, founding director, Keilty, Goldsmith and Company

"A positive and practical message for these times of increasing change and confusion."
>—DON PETRIE, adviser, Training and Development, Shell Canada Limited

"David Noer conveys concisely and clearly the important organizational and cultural needs that set apart the real winner. I would strongly encourage those with an enlightened view of what management responsibility *really* entails to read this book."
>—ROBERT A. INGRAM, president and CEO, GlaxoWellcome Inc.

From 1975 to 1982, he was the Senior Vice President, Personnel and Administration for Commercial Credit Company. Commercial Credit was a holding company with operating units in the insurance, finance, consumer lending, banking, leasing and real estate fields. In addition to the traditional human resource activities, he managed strategic planning, purchasing, public relations and data processing. Considerable effort was spent in divestiture and acquisition planning.

From 1965 to 1975, he held a number of increasingly responsible human resource positions in the United States, Europe and Asia. Dr. Noer resided in Melbourne, Australia for three years during this period and was responsible for human resource management and consulting throughout Asia.

He is the author of a wide range of popular articles and published research in consulting skills, individual and executive development, and international human resource management, and has written four books: *Multinational People Management: A Guide to Organizations and Employees* (BNA, 1974); *The Employment Game* (Chilton, 1975); *Jobkeeping: A Hireling's Survival Manual* (Chilton, 1976); *Healing the Wounds: Overcoming the Trauma of Layoffs and Revitalizing Downsized Organizations* (Jossey-Bass, 1993); and *Breaking Free: A Prescription for Personal and Organizational Change* (Jossey-Bass, 1996).

He received a B.A. from Gustavus Adolphus College, and a M.S. in Organizational Development from Pepperdine University. He earned a Doctorate in Business Administration with a concentration in Organizational Behavior, and a supporting field of Executive Mental Health from George Washington University. He served as a member of the governing board of the Organizational Development Network, and was editor of the journal, OD Practitioner.

DAVID M. NOER, D.B.A.

Dr. Noer's current speaking and research interests deal with the effects of layoffs and downsizing on those who remain in organizations, the revitalization of people in the workforce, and executive and team effectiveness.

Noer currently heads his own consulting and training organization in Greensboro, North Carolina. He has been designated an Honorary Senior Fellow of the Center for Creative Leadership, and was previously Senior Vice President for Training and Education with world-wide responsibility for the Center's training and educational activities.

Before joining the Center for Creative Leadership, he was President of his own consulting firm. His previous position was as Dean of the Control Data Academy of Management, and Vice President of Human Resource Development. He had world-wide responsibility for executive succession planning and top executive development. He also was responsible for human resource research, planning and organizational development strategies.

He served as President and CEO of Control Data Business Advisors. This involved P&L responsibility for a $60 million subsidiary of Control Data specializing in technology-based human resource oriented management consulting. This organization included Control Data's corporate human resource development, strategic planning, and market research staff, and provided products and consulting services through offices in the United States, London and Melbourne. In addition to managing the firm, Dr. Noer provided personal organization diagnostic and development consulting to top executives in a number of

BREAKING FREE

BREAKING FREE

A Prescription for Personal and Organizational Change

David M. Noer

Author of *Healing the Wounds*

Jossey-Bass Publishers

Chapter One: quotes from FOX IN SOCKS by Dr. Seuss TM and copyright © 1965 and renewed 1993 by Dr. Seuss Enterprises, L.P. Reprinted by permission of Random House, Inc., and International Creative Management, Inc., as agents for Dr. Seuss Enterprises, L.P.

Chapter Eight: quotes from "My Heroes Have Always Been Cowboys," written by Sharon Rice, are used by permission. Copyright © 1976 PolyGram International Publishing, Inc. All Rights Reserved.

Chapter Eight: use of WE SHALL OVERCOME. Musical and Lyrical adaptation by Zilphia Horton, Frank Hamilton, Guy Carawan, and Pete Seeger. Inspired by African American Gospel Singing, members of the Food & Tobacco Workers Union, Charleston, SC, and the southern Civil Rights Movement. TRO © Copyright 1960 (Renewed) and 1963 (Renewed) Ludlow Music, Inc., New York, International Copyright Secured. Made In U.S.A. All Rights Reserved Including Public Performance For Profit. Used by Permission.

Chapter Nine: quotes from THE LITTLE ENGINE THAT COULD—I THINK I CAN, I THINK I CAN—are trademarks of Platt & Munk, Publishers, and are used by permission.

Chapter Nine: quotes from "High Hopes," words by Sammy Cahn, music by James Van Heusen, are reprinted by permission of Warner Bros. Publications, Miami, FL 33014. Copyright © 1959 by Sincap Productions, Inc.; Copyright © 1959 by Maraville Music Corp. Copyright renewed by Maraville Music Corp. All rights reserved.

Chapter Ten: quotes from "Me and Bobby McGee," words and music by Kris Kristofferson and Fred Foster, are used by permission. © 1969 TEMI COMBINE INC. All rights controlled by COMBINE MUSIC CORP. and administered by EMI BLACKWOOD MUSIC INC. All rights reserved. International copyright secured.

For sales outside the United States, please contact your local Simon & Schuster International Office.

 Manufactured in the United States of America on Lyons Falls Pathfinder Tradebook. This paper is acid-free and 100 percent totally chlorine-free.

Library of Congress Cataloging-in-Publication Data

Noer, David M.
    Breaking free : a prescription for personal and organizational change / David M. Noer. — 1st ed.
        p.   cm. — (Jossey-Bass business & management series)
    Includes bibliographical references and index.
    ISBN 0-7879-0267-5 (alk. paper)
    1. Organizational change.   2. Organizational learning.   I. Title.
II. Series.
HD58.8.N63   1996
650.1—dc20   96-23951

FIRST EDITION
HB Printing   10 9 8 7 6 5 4 3 2 1

Contents

Preface

I recently asked a top manager to write a metaphorical story about his organization. Here is a condensed version of what he came up with: "We're like a bunch of ants clinging to a slippery log, careening down a raging, flood-swollen river. We're scrambling all over, having meetings, writing reports, pushing some of our fellow ants overboard, and all the while arguing about where we are going and who should steer! No matter how hard we try to control it, reengineer it, or downsize it, that log is going where it wants to go. I know there are lots of rocks and waterfalls downstream, and I'm not sure if either we remaining ants, or the log, are going to survive the trip."

His picturesque description outlines a new reality that is increasingly familiar to all of us who work in today's organizations. It is an environment that, too often, causes us to respond as passive victims and our organizations to turn inward and retreat into inappropriate control. It doesn't need to be that way. We don't have to be ants, centering our lives by doggedly hanging on to slippery and out-of-control logs, and our organizations do not have to speed, unmanaged, toward unseen hazards.

Breaking Free is about individual relevance and organizational survival. It offers hope and optimism, and frames what to most of us and our organizations is a crucial choice. We can pursue the path of learning and freedom, reclaim our self-esteem, and apply our human spirit to relevant and meaningful work in the service of others. Our organizations can break the dysfunctional ties of old-paradigm bureaucracy and reform into learning communities that will attract the type of employee who will ensure their future survival. This book unabashedly advocates the positive and affirming choice of individual and organizational freedom, and supports that advocacy by offering concrete, practical advice and guidelines.

Audience

Although *Breaking Free* will be of value to all who seek to understand the connection of person to organization in the new reality, I have written it with three often-overlapping audiences in mind: organizational managers and leaders; organizational employees; and consultants, academics, and change agents.

Organizational Managers and Leaders

If you are in a managerial or leadership role, you have a particularly important and difficult task. You must help your employees learn how to learn and your organization establish a learning culture. *Breaking Free* will help you in a number of concrete and specific ways. Chapters Two through Five will give you practical advice for understanding and dealing with your own and your employees' response to transition and change. Chapter Six provides guidelines for assessing your organization's response type, and Chapter Seven presents a series of practical worksheets that will facilitate your analysis of the relationship of your individual response type to that of your organization. Chapter Eight specifically focuses on new-reality leadership issues and the crucial competency of transition facilitation. Chapter Nine outlines a concrete model for increasing your learning and problem-solving tactics, and Chapter Ten gives you specific tips for helping individuals and organizations break free and pursue the learning path.

Organizational Employees

If you work in an organization and occupy a nonmanagerial role, it is very easy to conclude that the system is doing things to you and you have no control. That logic path will quickly lead you to the status of a victim—a condition you definitely want to avoid. *Breaking Free* will help you escape this victim mentality by giving you guidelines and ideas geared to let you take charge of your own fate. As is the case with organizational managers and leaders, the first seven chapters present you with a concrete process for understanding and dealing with your own and your organization's preferred patterns of responding to change and transition. You will find specific guidelines for moving toward—and maintaining—a learning response. The last three chapters will help you understand that leadership, learning, and the freedom choice are not solely reserved for those occupying managerial roles in the corporate organization chart. You will find ideas, tips, and examples, and most important, you will discover a path toward an optimistic and relevant future.

Consultants, Academics, and Change Agents

If, like me, you are involved in helping and studying organizational systems and the people who work in them, then—also like me—you no doubt thrive on the stimulation of new ideas and different models. If your bottom line is helping people become more relevant and organizations more productive, the ideas, models, and concepts found in *Breaking Free* will be of value to your work.

Overview of the Contents

The book is divided into four parts. Part One discusses how to deal with the new reality. Chapter One uses a senior team's struggle to understand and accommodate the new reality as a way to frame basic issues of loyalty, motivation, and commitment in the new reality. This group's quest for "the glue that holds the organization together" leads to an actual recipe for glue, which provides a metaphorical review of the bonding agents of the new reality. The chapter concludes with an introduction to the response factor model. This model, which outlines the differences people have in their capacity for changing (the ability to learn from experience), and their comfort with change (the readiness to learn), forms the structure for the next four chapters (Part Two).

Chapter Two deals with the response type (R-type) we call *overwhelmed*. This R-type has a low capacity for changing and a low comfort with change. Employees of this type are quite literally overwhelmed by the stress and trauma of organizational transition, and their primary response pattern involves withdrawing from the fray and avoiding the necessary learning and personal change. A large percentage of many new-reality workforces are made up of employees with the R-overwhelmed response pattern, so it is an important type to understand. This chapter not only describes how overwhelmed employees feel, react to transitions, and function as learners, but also what they need to successfully cope with change. It gives practical advice and offers guidelines to help them develop more useful coping behavior.

Chapter Three focuses on the *entrenched* response pattern. Entrenched employees have a high capacity for change and learning combined with a low comfort level. They react to change and transition by working very hard at old and often dysfunctional ways of solving problems. Their primary coping mechanism involves clinging tenaciously to narrow learning patterns that worked in the past. They are found in great numbers in certain types of industries, such as the new regional phone companies, the public utilities, government offices, and the military. They are found in abundance in certain staff groups who have been heavily invested in control and rules administration. The chapter not only provides insight into the world of the entrenched, but also practical advice and guidelines as to how to help them move toward more productive and personally meaningful ways of coping with change and transition.

In Chapter Four, we encounter that odoriferous character called the *BSer*. Those exhibiting the BS response have a high comfort with change and a low capacity for change. Their primary pattern involves a form of hipshooting aggressiveness. Their comfort with change, coupled with their lack of any need or desire to anchor that change in new learning or behavior, causes them to push for action without any grounding in theory or strategy. BSers tend to congregate in upper middle management and are dangerous because they are initially hard to spot and, when empowered, can lead an organization rapidly in the wrong direction. Through examples and case studies, readers are offered advice and strategies to both help rein in the power of employees exhibiting R-BS behavior, and tips to help move them into more productive response patterns.

Chapter Five deals with the *learning* response. Learners have a high comfort with change and an equally high ability to change. A workforce populated by people with the ability to learn how to learn offers the ultimate competitive advantage. Past chapters provided advice as to how to move the overwhelmed, entrenched, and BS response types toward the learning response. This chapter offers suggestions and ideas geared to keeping employees in a learning mode, protecting them from burnout, and creating organizational cultures that will attract and retain them.

Part Three shows how to relate individual and organizational R-types. Chapter Six shifts the focus from the individual to the organization. Organizations also, based on their culture and history, are predisposed to respond to change in one of the four response patterns. This chapter offers advice and ideas as to how to identify, cope with, and change organizations with overwhelmed, entrenched, and BS response patterns. The goal is the creation and maintenance of learning organizations.

Chapter Seven presents a set of worksheets that allows the reader to assess both individual and organizational response types. Guidelines are then provided for understanding and accommodating the fit between individual and organizational response patterns. This chapter provides a very practical and hands-on way of working with R-type analysis.

Part Four includes Chapters Eight, Nine, and Ten. In Chapter Eight, the focus shifts to leadership. Through examples and case studies, the chapter establishes that leadership is a shared process and that the true task of those in leadership roles in the new reality is transition facilitation. Again, in this chapter, the orientation is toward pragmatic advice, including a list of specific activities that will help develop transition facilitation skills.

Chapter Nine returns to the subject of learning, this time offering a practical model for developing a wider set of learning tactics. It outlines a process that enables readers to assess and map their individual learning tactics. The necessity to push individual learning against the grain of past individual and organizational conditioning is explained, and individuals and organizations are offered guidelines and ideas as to how to facilitate this painful but necessary process.

In Chapter Ten, the book concludes with a discussion of the need for both individuals and organizations to break free of the limiting and dysfunctional constraints of the past. The connection between individual and organizational freedom is emphasized in a section discussing the Yin-Yang dance of freedom and learning. Another section presents clear guidelines and practical ideas for individual behavior and organizational development oriented toward freedom. The chapter emphasizes the necessity for individuals to connect their self-esteem to what they do and not where they work, and for organizations to develop cultures where people come to work because they choose to be there, not because they have to be there.

There are two appendixes. Appendix A provides a frame of reference and a bridge to my previous book, *Healing the Wounds* (1993), and defines and provides examples of some of the common terms used in the book. Appendix B traces the development and evolution of the R-factor model.

Breaking Free pursues and connects several interrelated themes: the importance of learning how to learn as the only certain response to an ambiguous and confusing future, individual differences in the way we and our organizations cope with change and transition (the R-factor), the necessity of reconceptualizing the roles of our leaders and the process of leadership, and our—and our organizations'— need to break free of the limitations and constraints of the old reality. The path of freedom and learning leads to a breathtaking future of individual relevance and organizational productivity. We have no alternative but to take it.

Greensboro, North Carolina   DAVID M. NOER
July 1996

Acknowledgments

I am deeply indebted to my friend and colleague Kerry Bunker. Not only is his influence reflected in many of these pages but his spirit and wisdom continue to nourish me.

I need to acknowledge all the individuals and organizations whose real-life struggles and victories found their way into the stories and examples. They are reflective of those who strive each day to lead organizational lives of relevance, learning, and freedom. They are the true heroes of this book.

The library at the Center for Creative Leadership has been a valuable resource, and I particularly want to express my appreciation to Carol Keck and Peggy Cartner for their support and responsiveness. I want to thank two people at Jossey-Bass: Bill Hicks for his tenacity and Larry Alexander for his support. Both traits helped keep the book on track. A very special thanks to a very special person: Judy Turpin, whose organization, humor, word processing skills, and unique ability to translate my handwriting helped make the manuscript a reality. Above all, I want to thank my wife, Diana, for her patience, support, love, and—among sometimes trying circumstances—unconditional positive regard!

Finally, I need to say that although I worked for the Center for Creative Leadership during the preparation of the book, the opinions and ideas are mine and not necessarily shared by all my colleagues or representative of Center policy.

D.M.N.

The Author

DAVID M. NOER currently heads his own consulting and training organization in Greensboro, North Carolina. He has been designated an honorary senior fellow of the Center for Creative Leadership, where he previously was senior vice president for training and education, with worldwide responsibility for the Center's training and educational activities. His professional interests, apart from assistance to layoff survivors, are focused on breaking individuals' codependent relationships with organizations to create employee autonomy, peak effectiveness among executives, new-paradigm leadership, and healthier, more competitive organizations.

Before joining the Center for Creative Leadership, Noer was president of his own consulting firm, specializing in workforce revitalization, executive development, and strategic planning. Much of his work helped executive teams and organizational systems deal with the effects of layoffs on employees who remained behind.

Noer has also held positions as dean of the Control Data Academy of Management and as vice president of human resource development for the same organization, with responsibilities for succession planning, executive development, human resource research, and organizational development.

He has served as president and chief executive officer of Business Advisors, a Control Data subsidiary specializing in technology-based management consulting, with offices in the United States,

England, and Australia. In addition to managing the firm, Noer provided diagnostic and developmental organizational consulting to executives dealing with the human implications of restructuring, downsizing, and layoffs.

Noer has also served as senior vice president of personnel and administration for Commercial Credit Company, a holding company with operating units in the fields of insurance, finance, consumer lending, banking, leasing, and real estate. In addition, he has held line and staff positions in the United States, Europe, and Asia.

Noer is the author of many articles on consulting skills, individual and executive development, and international human resource management. He has written four other books: *Multinational People Management* (1975), *How to Beat the Employment Game* (1975), *Jobkeeping* (1976), and *Healing the Wounds* (1993).

He received his B.A. degree (1962) in psychology and history from Gustavus Adolphus College, his M.S. degree (1979) in organizational development from Pepperdine University, and his D.B.A. degree (1988), with a concentration in organizational behavior and a supporting field of executive mental health, from George Washington University.

He has served as adjunct faculty member at St. Thomas University and is a member of several professional associations. He also served on the board of trustees for the Organizational Development Network and was editor of the journal *OD Practitioner*.

BREAKING FREE

Part I

Struggling with the New Reality

1

The Quest for Glue

It was the first time I had seen a chief financial officer cry. Not that CFOs, or any occupational type, analytical or not, should be immune from the cleansing and humanizing release of tears; it just was the first time I'd seen it happen. And it took place in front of all of his top management colleagues, to boot!

It was late the second night. We'd been at it for one night and two full days. Everyone was tired and frustrated. The group—consisting of Charles, the CFO; his boss, the president; and his peers, the senior staff of a medium-sized high-technology manufacturing and sales organization—had been struggling to develop a transition plan. They had reluctantly conceded that they were looking at a permanent shift to what consultants and academics call the new paradigm or the new psychological contract, what the team more simply and directly called the new deal. The magnitude of this new deal had seeped into the collective consciousness of the group until, like an unchecked virus, it nearly suffocated them.

The framework of their way of experiencing this new deal, which they phrased in very terse and personal terms, was displayed on two pieces of newsprint taped to the wall. There were six points:

- *"Layoffs will continue."* This meant that they would continue taking out their friends and colleagues well into the future. In fact, they concluded that they couldn't predict an end.

- *"Even our jobs aren't safe."* There were two subcaptions under this main point, "He who lives by the sword, dies by the sword," which summarized a spirited discussion about their cost-cutting culture, and "We are all temps." These were difficult ideas to admit or for the team to publicly state in front of their boss.

- *"The old system is dead."* The relationship of person to organization that most of them had internalized was that the obligation of the good employee was to fit in and behave in accordance with organizationally sanctioned rules and standards, and the obligation of a good employer was to take care of a good employee over a forty-year career.

- *"We are not happy campers."* This was really hard for them to say and required prodding and hypothesis testing. If Charles's boss, the president, hadn't assembled a team that valued truth telling and encouraged an open climate, it never would have come out. Each of the team members admitted feeling some combination of anger, anxiety, and frustration. Had they worked on it a little longer, my guess was that feelings of guilt and depression would also have emerged. Based on the amount of alcohol consumed during that retreat, and stories of incredibly long and frustrating work hours resulting in little or no family life, it was apparent that the new deal was affecting more than their work lives.

- *"We don't know how to manage anymore."* The group concluded that they needed two very unique sets of skills to help turn their organization around. The first need was to help their employees respond to the debilitating effects of layoff survivor sickness—feelings just like theirs: anger, fear, guilt, and depression. They also needed a different approach for the small but highly productive group of employees who had decoupled their self-esteem from fitting into the internal bureaucracy and, instead, invested it in their work and serving their customers. Both leadership skill sets were new and certainly different than those they required in the past. These two distinct groupings of employees are in Charles's organization

representative of two of the four response types (R-types) we will
be exploring in much greater detail in later chapters.

- *"We're out of glue."* There was no apparent substitute—at
least to that group at that time—for what they characterized as the
glue that had held the old organization together. Even though they
by this time understood, at least in their heads, that tying employees' self-esteem into a long-term, internally oriented career would
no longer work, they didn't feel it where it counted: in their hearts.
Their heads told them to accept that the dawning of the new reality didn't make the old reality bad (it had served them and the organization well for many years), but their hearts were filled with a
sense of failure and depression. This was partially because of their
own unresolved layoff survivor sickness, and partially because they
were frustrated at looking for one quick fix for a very complex set
of issues. (Appendix A provides an overview of layoff survivor sickness and other concepts found throughout this book.)

It was this last point, the lack of glue, that caused Charles himself to become unglued. The group's energy level was on empty, they
couldn't do any more work that night, and for a long time, they sat,
quietly looking at the newsprint. Finally, Charles abruptly blurted
out, "Everything we worked so hard to build here has come apart."
Then, after a long, painful pause when you could hear everyone
breathing, he continued, this time very quietly and with increasing
emotion. "It just isn't fair!" he whispered. The tears had begun, and
he blew his nose. "How can we hold the place together?" he asked,
the tears flowing. "Where's the loyalty in this new deal? How can
we manage a bunch of mercenaries?" he lamented. "There's no glue
left to hold the organization together!"

Of Old Dogs and New Tricks

The pain felt by Charles's group was real, and the frustration they
experienced is increasingly shared by many organizational leaders

who came up under the old psychological contract, where people placed their self-esteem and sense of relevance in the organizational vault and the organization responded by taking care of them over a lifetime career. Their self-worth, their ideas about what constitutes loyalty and motivation, and their concepts of leadership were forged under a very different system from that in which they now operate. What got them there won't keep them or their organizations there. Yet it is very difficult to let go. As a wise and experienced CEO once said in his best Carolina drawl, "Old dawgs can learn new tricks, but it's damn hard! The old tricks is what let us get to be old dawgs in the first place!"

It is understandable for old dogs to feel sad and powerless when their old tricks don't make sense in the new world. The answer is brutally simple—to stay around and get to be even older dogs, they do need to learn newer tricks. Learning is the key, and the most basic learning is that there is, indeed, a new world. There are lots of juicy bones out there for those old dogs who have learned how to learn and can translate that process into organizational cultures that facilitate collective learning.

From Ties to Stickiness

As the old psychological contract between individual and organization continues to unravel, many of us are struggling with basic questions such as how to lead, motivate, and plan in this uncharted new environment—where, like it or not, we are all temporary employees. Tornow and DeMeuse (1990) capture the essence of the issue in the title of their article, "The Tie That Binds Has Become Very, Very Frayed." In my experience, most managers—like Charles—conceptualize this dilemma more in terms of stickiness than ties. The increasingly voiced question is, "After all the layoffs, early retirements, reengineering, and restructuring, what is the glue that will hold this organization together?"

Just what is this new glue and how can we use it without getting stuck in it? This subject of a new adhesive was addressed in the mid-sixties by none other than that great student of human behavior, Dr. Seuss, when he wrote through the voice of his *Fox in Sox* (Geisel, 1965, p. 31):

> We'll find something new to do now.
> Here is lots of new blue goo now.
> Gooey. Gooey.
> Blue goo. New goo.
> Gluey, Gluey.

From External to Internal: The New Adhesive

That Fox was on to something! There is lots of gooey stuff out there; it is rooted in human spirit, participation, and learning, and it is "Gluey, Gluey." Before we can apply his *new* goo, however, we need to tear ourselves away from the *old* glue, which was external and applied from the top down. This is replaced by the new adhesive, which is internal and self-administered.

The old glue, which did a good job of building and holding organizations together for the past fifty years, has lost its stickiness. In the Fox's words, it is no longer "Gooey." It was made up of largeness, hierarchy, bureaucracy, and upward mobility. Loyalty equated to fitting in and the major adhesive property was applied paternalism. This old glue no longer works and we need to stop relying on it and put our faith in the new stuff. There are five things we need to develop to let this new glue do its magic:

- Awareness that motivation and commitment are not irrevocably bound to lifetime employment, organizational loyalty, and fitting in.

- Understanding that it is possible—in fact essential for survival—to do excellent work in the service of others without a lifetime guarantee of employment, or placing all one's social, emotional, or financial eggs in the organizational basket.

- Awareness that organizational commitment and productivity are not diminished by loyalty to self, work-team, or profession.

- Understanding that leadership is very different in a liberated workforce unencumbered by fear, false expectations of promotions, or the distractions of politics and trying to impress the boss.

- Understanding of what is the most profound "gooey" learning, what I call the paradox of freedom.

When people stay in a personal relationship because they choose to be there and know they have a no-fault option of leaving; when armies are made up of volunteers and not conscripts; and when workers choose to stay in organizations because of the work and the customers, knowing they may not be able to stay for an entire career—they all tend to be much more productive and committed. The way the paradox of freedom relates to job security is that when people choose to stay for the right reasons (the work and the customer), as opposed to the wrong reasons (false expectations of long-term security), their job security tends to increase!

New Glue

The vision of Charles, the tearful chief financial officer, and his colleagues sitting in despair in front of two sheets of newsprint depicting their recently discovered disillusionment with the old reality causes me to take artistic license and add an empty glue pot to the picture. This imaginary glue pot is on the floor between the flip charts and the executives and the faded words *motivation* and *com-*

mitment are stenciled on its side. To complete the vision, a recipe for preparing the gooey stuff that will hold organizations of the future together is necessary.

The Recipe

FILL Glue Pot with the fresh, pure, clear water of undiluted human spirit . . .

- Take special care not to contaminate with preconceived ideas, or to pollute with excess control.
- Fill slowly; notice that the pot only fills from the bottom up. It's impossible to fill it from the top down!

STIR in equal parts . . .

- Customer focus.
- Pride in good work.

BRING to boil and blend in . . .

- A liberal portion of diversity.
- One part self-esteem.
- One part tolerance.

FOLD in . . .

- Accountability.
- Openness to learning.

SIMMER until smooth and thick, stirring with . . .

- Shared leadership and clear goals.

SEASON with . . .

- A dash of humor and a pinch of adventure.

LET cool and garnish with . . .

- A topping of core values.

> *SERVE by coating all boxes in the organization chart, with particular attention to the white spaces. With proper application, the boxes disappear and all that can be seen is productivity, creativity, and customer service.*

We have a choice: we can accept this new gooey glue or fight what will prove to be a frustrating battle that we will ultimately lose by attempting to hold today's organizations together with the non-sticky glue of the past. The new glue can be internalized, or, as the Fox says, "chewed." This ingestion is highly recommended, as it will develop the individual and organizational learning that is necessary for productivity and survival. The wise Fox speaks both of the choice we must make and of the process of ingestion (Geisel, 1965, p. 32).

> Do you choose to
> chew goo, too, Sir?
> If, Sir, you, Sir,
> choose to chew, Sir,
> with the Goo-Goose,
> chew, Sir. Do, Sir.

The Seductive Search for the Objective External Tool

Two aspects of the new glue cause many leaders great difficulty: it is applied from the inside out, and it is suspended in the extremely powerful but nonobjective wet, sticky, stuff of the human spirit. The path toward individual relevance and organizational learning is not linear. Breaking free and learning how to learn is a subjective, inside-out, messy process that is at odds with the avowed external, objective reality of the old paradigm. In truth, the flames of personal growth and insight have always been fanned by the internal, subjective winds of the human spirit. The process was just kept in the closet in the old paradigm.

Too many organizations are reacting to the future with the mantras of the past, approaching the task with a frenzy of activity. They are pursuing the futile quest for an objective, external tool with a fervor fueled by their need to ensure organizational survival. One frustrated leader described his organization's action frenzy as follows:

> First we decide we are going north and we get on a freeway and drive like hell—one hundred miles an hour. Then we come to an intersection and we decide to head east and we barrel off in that direction, but that doesn't seem to get us anywhere so we turn around and speed back west, and finally we decide to go back to basics and head south again as fast as we can drive! All the while we are debating who should steer as we watch the gas gauge moving toward empty!

The solution, as this person was eventually to discover, was that the answers were to be found inside the car, not in its destination. Figure 1.1 illustrates the frustration experienced by many leaders who have become painfully aware of the new reality and are seeking a single external lever to move the rock that is crushing their organizational creativity and competitiveness.

Unfortunately, there is no single tool that will move the rock. The answer as depicted in Figure 1.2 lies in learning and insight; in skills and perspectives that will shatter the rock from inside out.

The Seductive Pleasure of Shooting Snakes

Tempting though it may be, organizational leaders need to reject the temptation to look for one-dimensional external answers. They need the courage and fortitude to move from external solutions to internal insights. This is difficult, given the snake-shooting heritage of the old paradigm, with its perceived one-on-one relationship

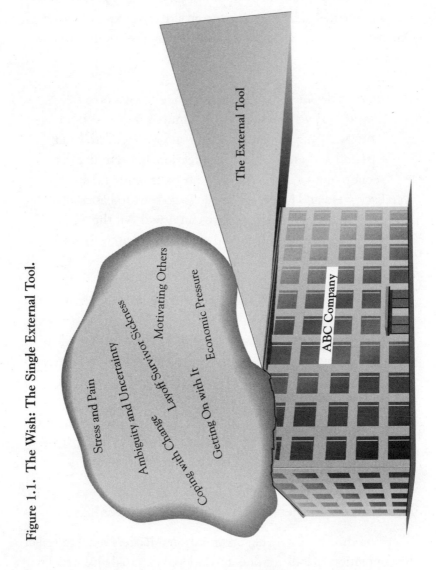

Figure 1.1. The Wish: The Single External Tool.

Stress and Pain

Ambiguity and Uncertainty

Motivating Others

Layoff Survivor Sickness

Coping with Change

Getting On with It

Economic Pressure

The External Tool

ABC Company

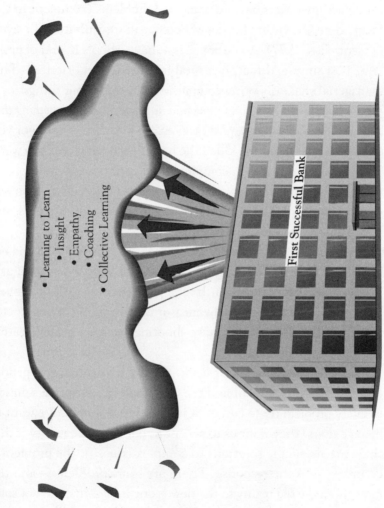

Figure 1.2. The Reality: Relief Comes from Inside Out.

- Learning to Learn
  - Insight
  - Empathy
  - Coaching
- Collective Learning

First Successful Bank

between problems and solutions. Consultant Pat Williams, a connoisseur of things Western, uses the metaphor of a group of cowboys sitting around an evening campfire and telling tales of the rattlesnakes they shot during the day to illustrate the knee-jerk reaction many managers have to perceived problems (comment to the Pepperdine University Master of Science in Organizational Development class, 1977). A cowboy sees a snake, shoots it, end of problem! It is simple, direct, measurable, and action oriented. This managerial snake-shooting compulsion illustrates four things:

• *Snake shooting is a simple and direct response, something that can be measured and rewarded.* You either killed the snakes or you didn't, and the more you killed the better problem solver you were. This is a system that is in complete sync with the external, objective nature of many old-paradigm measurement systems. It is an orientation upon which a number of compensation systems and management theories have been based.

• *Management by killing snakes deals with the symptom and not the disease.* Killing snakes is not a good idea for the system as a whole. Snakes are on this earth for a purpose and fit into the overall ecological system. Thus, by measuring, rewarding, and perpetuating myths and cultures of snake shooting, we are actually creating a much bigger problem.

• *Simple solutions don't work.* As much as those who peddle one-minute management and the one single, prescriptive solution to every problem try to con us, it just isn't that simple. We want to believe it and they want us to accept it, but the basic reality is that there are no simple solutions to complex issues! If the problem is complex, so is the response. There are some problems—and the move from the old reality to the new is one itself—that are not solution oriented and can only be dealt with at the level of accommodation. In the old paradigm, there was a bias against complexity. Otherwise intelligent and inquisitive managers colluded in the simplistic fiction that there was a linear, one-on-one relationship between problems and solutions: all problems had solutions and the task of a good manager was to solve problems.

- *Systemic thinking is harder, deeper, and better.* Snakes need to be accommodated, not eradicated, and the talk around the fire needs to be moved from braggadocio and storytelling to dialogue and learning. The conversation needs to be about ways to live with snakes, ways to accept and accommodate their existence as opposed to tales of how they are killed. This demands very different myths and reward systems. It requires new theories and models of management and leadership. Leading the liberated, task-focused, and essentially temporary employee of the new reality requires a much more complex set of skills than managing the snake shooters of the old reality.

You Are the Tool

The futile quest for an external, objective tool is a dysfunctional heritage of the old paradigm; the outgrowth of the erroneous attempt to graft the objectivity of the scientific method onto the subjective phenomena of the human spirit. It is a fundamental mismatch. In a time when even such previously objective bastions of the old science as Newtonian physics have had their subjective dark side exposed, many organizational leaders continue to seek objective solutions to subjective problems.

Although there are a number of techniques and processes—the philosophy of quality, the focus on small groups and teams, and new status and reward systems—flourishing in the new reality, the primary tool is the manager as an individual. The manager's ability to learn how to learn, along with his values, self-insight, and helping skills are the foundation of productive new-paradigm organizations. The quest for the objective, external fix is a way of escaping the necessary pain of working internally. The basic receptacle of the new glue is the warm body of the individual employee. For it is the spirit, self-insight, and compassion of the individual that will facilitate the necessary individual and organizational learning that will lead to individual fulfillment and organizational productivity.

Plot Thickeners

As we move further into the new reality, it becomes clear that objective, external solutions are not the answer. The new glue is made up of warm, wet, sticky, nonlinear stuff; the only real tool lies in the application of our human spirit. Most of us need a frame of reference, a set of guidelines that will help us facilitate individual and organizational change in this ambiguous environment. This book provides a number of concrete and practical suggestions. First, however, it is necessary to review four additional plot thickeners:

- *Individual differences.* We are not all the same. While nearly all surviving employees experience feelings of violation and manifest symptoms of layoff survivor sickness (Appendix A), there are individual variations in symptom type and recovery prognosis.

- *Unending transitions.* We are, and will continue to be, in what Peter Vaill (1989, p. 1) describes as "permanent white water." There is white water as far as we can see into the future. The initial layoffs were the wake-up call for many individuals and organizations, but they were only the beginning. Our future reality is unending transitions.

- *Centrality of learning.* We can't possibly know all we need to know to navigate that eternal river of rapids in front of us. The best we can do is to develop individuals who have learned how to learn, and organizations that are able to learn in the collective.

- *New leadership orientation.* Leadership in the new reality is very different from leadership in the bureaucratic model of the past. Leadership is much more of a shared process than something that one person does to another. Those in formal leadership roles must be competent in the core task of leadership in the new reality: facilitating transitions—their own and those of their organizations.

The Response Factor Model

People vary in their reaction to change and transition. They require different strategies to move them toward the necessary learning response. These variations fit one of four patterns, which I call the response factors or R-factors. (Appendix B provides a review of the genealogy of this model.)

The R-factor model weaves together the four plot-thickening agents: individual differences, unending transitions, centrality of learning, and new leadership orientation. This model is of great value in helping to conceptualize the dynamic forces involved in moving toward the learning response and breaking free. (Although the examples in this and the next four chapters deal with individual response patterns, the model can also be applied to organizations. This organizational focus is discussed in Chapter Six.)

People vary in their capacity for changing (the ability to learn from their experience), and their comfort with change (the readiness to learn). As can be seen from Figure 1.3, there are four distinct response patterns and transition behaviors.

- *Low comfort with change, low capacity for change*. Individuals with this response pattern are called *overwhelmed*. Their primary transition behavior is to withdraw from the fray and avoid the necessary learning.
- *Low comfort with change, high capacity for change*. Those with this response are called *entrenched*. Their basic transition behavior involves tenaciously clinging to narrow learnings that worked in the past but are of limited value in the new reality.
- *High comfort with change, low capacity for change*. People of this response type are called *BSers* because they con themselves and others. Their transition behavior is made up of aggressive hip-shooting grounded in high drive and low substance.
- *High comfort with change, high capacity for change*. This is the *learner* type. The primary transition behavior of the learner involves positively dealing with the change (engaging), and learning new, more relevant skills (growing).

The Quest for Glue: Perspective and Observations

The times, they are a-changin'—and that change is not predictable, comfortable, or even very safe. Organizational leaders attempting to hold their organizations and themselves together during this

Figure 1.3. The R-Factor.

paradigm shift are understandably frustrated. With everything changing, the search for the glue that holds the organization together is a nontrivial pursuit.

The new glue is all about applied human spirit and learning. For it to work, organizational leaders need to change some deep-seated beliefs concerning the nature of motivation, commitment, and loyalty. It requires leaders to drop the seductive but futile search for an external, objective technique or tool that will alleviate the pain and stress of transition. The new glue works from the inside out and leads, not to an objective solution, but to insight and the learning response.

Organizations of the future will be characterized by unending transitions. Leadership processes will be needed that will result in the development of people who have learned how to learn and organizational systems with the capacity for collective learning. The Response Factor provides a means to conceptualize the dynamic forces involved when developing the necessary individual and organizational learning response. This model will provide the structure for the next several chapters.

Part II

Dealing with Change
The R-Factor Types

2

The Overwhelmed

Those who dwell in the lower left quadrant of the model are overwhelmed by the stress, change, and trauma of organizational change. On the horizontal axis, they find themselves unable to let go of the old, and even though they may be able to articulate the new reality and new ways of connecting with and contributing to the organization, they are unable to make it happen for themselves. On the vertical axis, they not only won't let go of the old ways, they can't! They are so locked into old patterns of organizational behavior they have lost their capacity to adapt and to learn from experience. They don't know how to learn how to learn.

As depicted in Figure 2.1, those with the overwhelmed response are underwater and sinking! If they don't do something they will drown. This metaphor is very appropriate. At one level, it is manifested in a suffocating form of victimhood. At another, it is found in self-destructive behavior emanating from bruised self-esteem and long-term depression. It results in abusive behavior toward both self and others. The tragedy of dwelling in this box too long is that it can result in permanent damage to that most precious and fundamental of all ingredients in the new glue: human spirit.

The primary response (R-behavior) of the overwhelmed involves withdrawing and avoiding. Overwhelmed employees withdraw from the fray although they often take potshots from the

Figure 2.1. The Overwhelmed: Low Comfort with Change, Low Capacity for Change.

The Overwhelmed

Withdrawing
and
Avoiding

sidelines. They avoid the necessary learning and personal change, hoping—without a lot of faith—that somehow "things will return to normal." Living in the lower left box is neither a happy nor productive time, as is illustrated by what nearly became the watery grave of Herman.

Herman's Wet Descent

I first discovered Herman in a smoke-filled conference room in Brussels. It was an uncomfortable meeting because of the heat and smoke. (Although it is not unusual for smoking to be allowed in European business meetings, the absence of any form of ventilation during a rare warm spell was not typical.) It was also uncomfortable because, in the midst of all the heat and smoke, the meeting itself was inauthentic. The participants consisted of a transition team of middle managers chartered to make recommendations as to how to put the pieces back together after a very traumatic merger. One result of putting these two organizations together was a large number of people reductions, or as Herman, who worked in one merger partner's U.K. operations called them, "redundancies."

It was one of those meetings where everyone was polite, analytical, detached, and low-key. Beneath the surface, most of them were anxious and mad as hell! This was a very traditional and ritualized organization, and, as we shall see, anger is more associated with the R-entrenched pattern than with the overwhelmed response. Herman, however, stood out in that group; his anger was turned inward. He thus demonstrated a key distinguishing factor of the overwhelmed: he was moving toward depression.

Herman, as one of the more senior members of the transition team, carved out his space at the head of the table. He was very quiet and his meeting behavior consisted of reserved and banal compliance. He would occasionally break out in a round of hacking coughing from within his encircling camouflage of smoke. He was a chain smoker at the time of the meeting.

That night, after the meeting, he held court in the bar. "It's bloody hopeless!" he complained to two other team members from "his half" of the new organization. The target of his anger were those from the "other half." "We're never going to get this place turned around! They have screwed it up. We need to get them out of there. Get someone who can get us back to our core business, back to normal!"

Herman's outburst in the bar that night demonstrated two additional characteristics of the R-overwhelmed: passive-aggressive behavior (low-key compliance in the meeting and angry blaming in the bar), and a strategy of wanting things to change, to get back to the way they were before the pain.

What Herman saw as needing to change were external things— the organizational leadership, the product offerings, and the way decisions were made on people assignments after the merger; never his own values and behavior.

I next saw Herman about six months later at a company meeting in London. He had lost weight, looked rumpled and disheveled, and the few comments he offered at the meeting were delivered with an affect that was flat, and a content that was incoherent. This was in sharp contrast to the old Herman, who was always immaculate and if anything overdressed. He had always been a terse, logic-based, nearly Spock-like, facts-only communicator.

His boss told me that Herman, "always one to like a drop," had crossed the line and was clearly in the grips of alcohol addiction. His past deliberate and analytical style was not valued in the new organization—it got in the way of the new risk-taking, market-driven culture. "He's depressed, drinks too much, bitches about everything, and hasn't a clue how to fit into the new organization. Too bad, he had lots of talent if only he could have learned to cope with the changes," the boss continued. "I've got to get him out of the organization."

Herman was sinking deep into the world of the R-overwhelmed; unable to learn new behaviors, and unwilling to let go of the past!

That was the last time I saw Herman. I have, however, heard from some of his colleagues who have remained in the consolidated organization. They reported some good news. He finally hit bottom, went through alcohol counseling and rehabilitation, and has surfaced as, of all things, an executive search consultant! He may have finally found a way to both capitalize on his past experiences and pass that hard-earned learning on to others in his new headhunting role.

Herman, although a classic case, is but one of many who dwell in the overwhelmed quadrant. Some clients have estimated that 50 to 60 percent of their workforce have done some time in this overwhelmed quadrant. One organization estimates a continuing hard core of from 30 to 40 percent. It is my experience that many organizations, in their movement toward the new reality, have permanently stranded a substantial number of employees in the troubled waters of the overwhelmed. Although I am always developmentally optimistic, the hard truth is that once people reach a certain depth in the overwhelmed water, they, like Herman, need to hit bottom and resurface in another organizational environment before they have a chance of snapping out of it. Self-esteem and a vital, risk-taking, energized human spirit are fragile commodities and are at peril for the truly overwhelmed.

The Overwhelmed: Four Dimensions

What follows is a review of four perspectives of the R-overwhelmed: their feelings, their typical reactions to transitions, their learning behavior, and what they need to be successful survivors. I will include some typical descriptions offered by clients and program participants.

How Overwhelmed Employees Feel

Somewhere between unhappy and depressed. Overwhelmed employees are, if not depressed, moving toward depression. They have a serious problem and don't know how to deal with it. Their initial anger soon turns inward, takes a toll on their self-esteem, and becomes depression. Typical descriptions of this feeling are:

> "She doesn't have any energy, she seems flat."
>
> "He is always sad. He used to be optimistic, but now he doesn't show any hope for himself or those who work for him."
>
> "He is beyond cynical—I just want to get away from him. His attitude is contagious."

Frustrated and anxious. They are frustrated because they are blocked both in letting go of the old ways and in learning the new ways. They hope things will change, but know they won't. They therefore know they don't fit in and that causes them a great deal of anxiety. Typical descriptions are:

> "He isn't making it in the new organization and he knows it. It really bothers him that we can't turn back the clock."
>
> "He sees every change as a job threat!"
>
> "I can't count on her to pull her weight—she fights everything we are trying to do but doesn't offer any options."

Bruised self-esteem. The behavior and learning patterns that got them where they are won't keep them there or move them forward. Since they are aware of the problem but are both unable and unwilling to deal with it, they judge themselves to be inadequate. Typical descriptions:

> "He is really down on himself. I couldn't give him that new project, he doesn't have any confidence."
>
> "I've now reached a point where I have to keep her away from customers."
>
> "He has lost his 'can do' attitude."

Powerless. The citizens of the R-overwhelmed quadrant are professional victims. By withdrawing, avoiding, and sinking into the overwhelmed sea, they give up their organizational power, and more important, their power over themselves. Typical descriptions:

> "She has dropped out, there is no sense of purpose."
>
> "He is waiting for things to get back to 'normal,' and that just isn't going to happen."
>
> "The job is running him—he's not running it!"

In need of approval and reassurance. Without any sense of personal control or direction, overwhelmed employees seek external validation. Typical descriptions:

"He always needs strokes even when he doesn't deserve them."

"I'm tired of telling her things are okay. I don't know if they are okay or not, but she doesn't want to hear that."

"He doesn't need a boss, he needs a motivational speaker every morning!"

Fearful of mistakes and failure. Because overwhelmed employees are unable to do anything positive for themselves or the organization, they attempt to minimize anything that could turn out negative. Typical descriptions:

"He won't take any risks."

"These organization changes have really pumped up his conservative streak."

"She is running scared."

In need of stability and symptom relief. Survivors in the R-overwhelmed quadrant want the pain to go away. They seek relief from the symptom and not the disease by wishing the organization would go back to the way it was when they felt better. Typical descriptions:

"He wants to turn the clock back."

"I really can't make her feel better—things are going to get worse before they improve."

"The roller coaster will just keep going faster—some of them just don't want to hear that."

How Overwhelmed Employees React to Transitions

Avoid confronting the real issues. The primary coping strategy of the overwhelmed employee is to ignore and block out the necessary personal and organizational changes. Typical descriptions:

"He doesn't get it! We need to speed up cycle time, not do it the same old way."

"She knows it's only a matter of time before she is out of here, but she keeps coming to work as though nothing has changed."

"He has got to stop writing memos and talk to us. Writing long memos is not the way to communicate today—no one has time to read them anyway."

Retreat into old patterns that are perceived as safe. Since overwhelmed employees are unable to learn the new ways and unwilling to let go of the old, a key coping strategy involves finding activities that fit with the old ways of doing things and are seen as safe. In reality they are not safe; they take time that could better be spent learning the new skills and processes. Typical descriptions:

"She writes out all her letters, then gives them to a secretary to type. I don't know why she doesn't learn to use the new word processing system. It would save her time and cut down on clerical expenses."

"He is the most organized man in the department—all his expense reports are in on time, his paperwork is perfect. Too bad we don't pay him for that. He needs to be less efficient in the office and get out there with the customers!"

Wait for things to return to normal. The residents of the lower left quadrant have a dim and fleeting hope that, somehow, things will return to what they remember as normal. Typical descriptions:

"She has gone through the new quality training, but I know she doesn't believe it. She's just going through the motions. I think she feels it will go away."

"He needs to get off his ass and start looking for another job. I can't understand why he ignores all the signs and just comes to work each day as though nothing has changed."

Engage in passive-aggressive behavior. The confusion, frustration, and anxiety of the overwhelmed employee is often acted out in behavior patterns that swing from passive compliance to externalized anger. Typical descriptions:

"She told all her employees that she supported the venting sessions, and the next day she told me how stupid they were."

"He says he agrees with the new structure in concept, then he attacks all the details—I'm not sure where he stands."

"He sings one song in the meetings and whistles a very different tune in the hallways."

Avoid thinking about or planning for the future. By withdrawing and avoiding, the overwhelmed employee escapes looking at the consequences of behavior. Typical descriptions:

"She needs to get out of that corporate staff role or she is out of here. It doesn't look like she is doing much!"

"If he doesn't get with the new customer service program he will be just another barrier to our success. He needs to help us find a solution, not be part of the problem."

"I don't know where she is taking our department. It seems like we just react and never commit to a course of action."

How Overwhelmed Employees Operate as Learners

Avoid and block necessary learning. The tragedy of the overwhelmed response pattern is that it blocks the necessary learning that will help both the individual and the organization. By withdrawing and avoiding, the employee runs away from the pain and struggle that are necessary to learn to do things differently and take responsibility for individual and organizational survival. Typical descriptions:

> "She doesn't take any responsibility for making this a better place."

> "He just lays back and waits for someone to tell him what to do. Hell, no one knows what to do, but some of us are out there trying to find answers."

> "I think he has given up trying to find a way to make it work. Since he is our supervisor, we just have to figure it out without him."

Equate activity with learning. A characteristic of those exhibiting the R-overwhelmed response is that they spend a lot of their energy attempting to look busy. This results in a dissipation of the overwhelmed employee's already limited reservoir of energy, and often the generation of activity that gets in the way of the real work of the system. Typical descriptions:

> "Since the restructuring, all our department has done is turn out volumes of useless reports that no one reads, and if someone makes a mistake and does read one, they don't find any information that will help them anyway."

> "I wish my boss would stop trying to help me by telling me what I need. I know what I need to move my group forward. I wish he would ask me. He needs to work around my needs, not his need to be useful in troubled times."

> "He holds planning meetings, strategy meetings, even meetings to plan meetings. It fills up the day, but I really can't see how that helps the customer."

Engage in patterns of abusive behavior. An outgrowth of the frustration stemming from withdrawal and blocked learning is a pattern of self-abuse and abuse of others. Employee assistance programs are booming. Excess drinking, drug abuse, overeating, and lack of exercise are examples of unhealthy coping. Unfortunately, the frustration also spills over into family and interpersonal relationships. I don't have hard data, but both anecdotal evidence and logic would predict an increase in spouse and child abuse. Typical descriptions:

> "He is drinking way too much these days."
>
> "I don't know what is going on at home, but based on what I see and hear, things can't be going too well for her there either."

Block the learning of others. Overwhelmed employees tend to both recruit others to join them on their sinking ship, and to get in the way of those attempting to implement the necessary individual and organizational change. Typical descriptions:

> "He will go to lunch with someone and when they return they both have new things to feel bad about!"
>
> "I need to get her out of my group. She gets in the way of what we need to do."
>
> "He is toxic to our change efforts!"

What Overwhelmed Employees Need to Be Successful Survivors

Help in dealing with stress, fear, and frustration. Those who reside in the R-overwhelmed box are badly in need of symptom relief. In terms of the pyramid model described in Appendix A (Noer, 1993), they need lots of level-two work: facilitated grieving and stress relief. Here it is a matter of treating the symptom first, then the disease. Unless overwhelmed employees gain symptom relief, they will never be able to make the necessary changes and be productive in the new reality. Helping overwhelmed employees is time intensive and does not offer the immediate bang for the buck that comes with working with the other large category: R-entrenched. Unfortunately, some organizations have come to the conclusion that the pain of working with employees exhibiting the R-overwhelmed pattern is not worth the gain. Ideas for intervention:

- Facilitated venting sessions, designed to get repressed feelings and emotions on the table.

- Individual counseling sessions, designed to move overwhelmed employees toward personal responsibility— and often to prepare them for leaving the organization.

- Clear and measurable performance standards with built-in feedback and coaching by a competent boss.

Competent leaders and peers who are willing to help calm the waters. There are two issues here. First, organizational leaders must possess the requisite counseling, feedback, and empathy skills. Second, they must have the time and energy to devote to dealing with the symptoms of the overwhelmed. There is a scarcity of both in most organizations. Bosses and peers often do not have counseling and empathy skills, and those who do are very busy people! Ideas for intervention:

- Incorporate venting, counseling, and realistic career expectations into the normal performance appraisal system.

- Train line managers in basic helping skills and require them to meet one-on-one with all their employees.

- Establish a peer counseling and performance appraisal process.

Phased-in transitions with success-loaded mini challenges. To regain a sense of control and experience success in the new reality, the overwhelmed employee needs carefully constructed activities that bridge from the comfortable old to the frightening new. These activities and experiences need to be loaded to ensure a high probability of success. When the success happens, the employee needs a great deal of positive feedback and recognition. The crafting of these experiences is labor intensive and requires both creativity and a large number of low-risk–high-reward projects. In the lean and focused world of the new reality there are not nearly as many of these opportunities as in the past. Since the same strategy also works well for the R-entrenched, many well-meaning organizational leaders are faced with hard choices over who participates in a limited number of this type of developmental assignment. Ideas for intervention:

- Serve on a task force or a special project with a large number of optimistic learners. Despite withdrawal, the overwhelmed employee can be pulled up and energized by the group.

- Assign to a project or a task force where the knowledge of the old system and the old ways are very important to designing the new.

- Serve on an external project such as the United Way where visibility is high and success is recognized.

- Transfer a limited number of high-potential overwhelmed employees (who haven't sunk too far) to a manager with coaching and development competencies. These assignments can be temporary and non–task-specific with the intention of the new boss crafting a number of success-loaded developmental tasks.

Encountering the Overwhelmed: Up Close and Personal

What follows are some practical tips for interacting with bosses and employees who are overwhelmed. I have also included some thoughts on what to do if you suspect that you, too, reside in the camp of the overwhelmed.

If You Work for One

If your boss is a resident of the R-overwhelmed box, you can do one or more of the following:

• Try to help through empathy, nonjudgmental listening, and feedback. This will not move the boss out of the overwhelmed category, but it can help alleviate the symptoms and start some movement in the right direction. Although being a counselor and coach to your supervisor is always a bit awkward, it is a strategy that has the best chance of success with an overwhelmed boss. Someone who is being sucked under by a quicksand of confusion and maladjustment will often latch on to a lifeline, regardless of the organizational level of the person on the other end.

• Review your situation against the four conditions necessary for success, and try to improve any that are within your reach.

> There must be mutual trust between the overwhelmed boss and the coaching subordinate.
>
> The boss must be salvageable, not have descended too deeply into the mire of withdrawal and avoidance.
>
> The coach cannot be overwhelmed too.
>
> The employee doing the coaching needs the requisite interpersonal skills.

• Ignore the boss and get on with your own transition. Although it may seem cruel to let someone else sink while you look after yourself, it is a very realistic and functional strategy. We are all, at times, temporary residents in the territory of the R-overwhelmed. The trick is to get out of Dodge as fast as possible. The way to do that is to let go of the old ways and learn how to adjust to the new reality. This is an adjustment that requires a significant investment of

energy. It is, for example, difficult to move from an internal orientation to a focus on external customers and to survive a reengineering
effort that takes out entire levels and comfortable old processes,
while at the same time attempting to rescue a boss who is overwhelmed. It may be best for you, the organization, and ultimately
the boss as well to let go and move on with your life.

•   Find a way to get out of the boss's jurisdiction if you can't
ignore or work around the problem. This could mean an internal
transfer or moving entirely out of the organization. The worst
choice—assuming you can not find a way to manage your own transition and do your job by remaining in your organization and ignor-
ing or working around your boss—is to stay in the reporting
relationship. This is unacceptable because there is the potential of
being pulled down into the depths of the overwhelmed waters along
with your boss. That is a stark prospect and an unacceptable risk!

If One Works for You

If you have one or more people reporting to you who exhibit R-
overwhelmed behavior patterns you have your work cut out for you!
From a productivity standpoint, your organizational work is not
getting done; overwhelmed employees are unable to make the
transition and cope by withdrawing and avoiding. From a people-
management standpoint, you have some very needy and energy-
draining people holding on to your coattails at a time when you need
all your stamina to deal with meeting competition or turning the
organization around. You have some choices:

•   *You can help your overwhelmed employees by attempting to save
them for the organization.* The primary activity is symptom relief.
The next step is finding carefully crafted and success-loaded assignments that bridge between their old reality and the new paradigm
in your organization. The downside of this is that it takes your
energy, organizational resources, and that most precious of all commodities—time!

• *You can help your overwhelmed employees by moving them out of the organization.* By providing counseling, feedback, and realistic career assessment during the outplacement effort you create three potential winners: the employee, the new employer, and your existing organization.

• *You can ignore them.* The good news is that in the short term, this frees up your energy to manage your own and your organization's transition. The bad news is that they won't go away. Even if you can afford the cost—financial and emotional—of keeping them around, they eventually need to be dealt with and you are back to the choice between helping them or getting rid of them. It is a pay me now or pay me later proposition!

If You Are One

If you suspect that you have taken up permanent residence in the R-overwhelmed box, you too have some options:

• Check your self-diagnosis: seek feedback. Find someone you trust and who respects you enough to tell you the truth. Go through the descriptions in this chapter (feelings, reactions to transitions, and operational mode as a learner). You may not have an accurate reading on yourself and you may be pleasantly surprised. On the other hand, you may indeed be overwhelmed.

• Try not to feel bad about feeling bad! Although it is not a pleasant place to be, it is impossible for any human to go through the wrenching changes in our organizational homes without doing some time in the overwhelmed box. Your task is to get out of the swamp as soon as you can. You don't want it to feel like home!

• Get some help. Start with the symptoms. You have got to get your feelings and emotions out and on the table before you can move on.

• Don't get too comfortable in the swamp. Some prisoners develop an institutional personality, they prefer life behind bars and can not handle freedom. If you stay in the overwhelmed swamp of withdrawal and avoidance too long, you will have a problem with your own organizational freedom and empowerment! Don't be afraid to leave the organization. It is often the first ring of a wonderful wake-up call.

• Take the time to learn. People who jump from one marriage or relationship to another without taking the time to learn why the first one didn't work usually repeat their mistakes. This is the classic rebound relationship. Don't be a rebound R-overwhelmed. Take the necessary learning and growth time in what Bridges (1980) calls the neutral zone.

The Overwhelmed: Perspective and Observations

Overwhelmed employees are the walking wounded in organizational transitions. They are forged by the human trauma following the inexorable move of organizations toward the new reality. They are found in surprisingly large numbers in all types of organizations: business, education, clergy, nonprofit, and military. Some organizations estimate that nearly a third of their workforce exhibits sustained R-overwhelmed behavior patterns.

Although the large number of overwhelmed employees is initially surprising, it is more understandable when one considers the persistence and the power of the three major factors that collude to produce R-overwhelmed patterns. The first is that our educational institutions reward conformity and often punish experimentation and collaboration. Jerry Harvey, creator of the *Abilene Paradox*, poses some interesting questions to his fellow educators in a fascinating article with the provocative title "Encouraging Students to Cheat: One Thought on the Difference Between Teaching Ethics and Teaching Ethically."

Does it strike you as odd, though, that virtually all educational institutions in our culture, from kindergarten through college, define cheating as "giving aid to others or receiving aid from them?" More specifically, does it

strike you as unusual that we define cheating as an act
of helping or being helped by others? Does it seem in
any way peculiar to you that an expression of altruism
has become an avatar of behavior that is immoral, dis-
honorable, and sullied? Alternatively, does it not strike
you as bizarre that, by defining cheating as the process
of helping others, we implicitly are saying that not being
helpful, that being narcissistic and selfish, is a proto-
typical expression of academic decency—and honor
[1984, p. 1].

The second major factor that contributes to the overwhelmed
response pattern is the powerful conditioning old-paradigm organizations exerted on their employees. Fitting in, being predictable,
conforming, honoring the old and reliable ways of doing things—
those are strong messages that don't die just because of a merger, a
change in customer preference, or the turn of an economy.

The final factor is the fact that organizations are as much social
systems as economic entities. People's sense of self-identity, purpose,
and role are strongly influenced by organizational systems. If who
you are is where you work, there is a lot more than a paycheck at
risk if your job is threatened! When we ask people to experiment,
collaborate, let go of the old ways of doing things, and perceive their
job as an economic rather than a social relationship, we are asking
a great deal. We are asking people to go against the grain of very
deep and tenacious patterns of cultural conditioning!

Although many overwhelmed employees can be turned around
and moved toward productive and contributing employment relationships, there is a point where some seem to sink below the point
of no return. They become so overwhelmed that the only hope
seems to be leaving the organization, spending substantial regenerative time in the neutral zone Bridges (1980) describes, and eventually reemerging in a different organizational system. I call this
hard-core group the outward-bound overwhelmed.

The primary strategy for helping the overwhelmed is symptom relief. In the next chapter, we shall discuss those who reside in the box of the R-entrenched. For these employees, the basic task involves letting go of old, ingrained values and patterns of work.

3

The Entrenched

Entrenched employees reside in the upper left corner of the R-factor model—and they live there a long time! That's why they are called entrenched. They have the ability to learn and change; they just have a hard time doing it. They don't, as do those who are overwhelmed, cope by withdrawing and avoiding. Entrenched employees react to change, transition, and organizational trauma by working extremely hard at old and often dysfunctional ways of solving problems. On the vertical axis, they have a high capacity to learn, and on the horizontal axis, they have low comfort and readiness. They are stuck in a fundamental mismatch: they attempt to cope with the new reality by using old techniques. As can be seen in Figure 3.1, their primary coping mechanism is to cling, often tenaciously, to narrow, constraining, and often dysfunctional learnings. They have learned how to cope so well in the old paradigm, they refuse to apply different, less limiting, and more productive processes that better fit their new reality.

Unlike the overwhelmed, those who cope with organizational transition with R-entrenched behavior patterns are often productive. However, they severely suboptimize their—and their organization's—potential. Because employees who respond to transitions with more openness and adaptivity are significantly more productive and creative, those with entrenched behavior patterns are constantly in danger of being replaced. Although entrenched employees

Figure 3.1. The Entrenched: Low Comfort with Change, High Capacity for Change.

The Entrenched

Clinging
to
Narrow
Learnings

frequently perform work that is useful to the organization, they do it in ways that are very narrow and limiting. At the same time, they expend much more energy than is necessary. A manager once described an entrenched colleague as "doing a quarter of what he needed to do by working ten times as hard as he should!"

The Perils of Playing for It

George has played the game of golf for over thirty years and has always had a basic flaw in his swing plane. He moves the club from outside in, causing the ball to spin to the right: a condition golfers call a fade when it doesn't go too far to the right, or a slice if it balloons way out. When he was younger, George adjusted by "playing for it." He spent a lot of time practicing aiming to the left and restraining the arc of his swing. The result was that he landed in the open much of the time, but he sacrificed a lot of distance and did not have any real control over where the ball ended up, losing the ability to strategically position his ball for the next shot.

During most of his golfing career, George played on a relatively short and wide-open public course. The people he played with were a combination of those who were just learning the game, people who were not serious golfers, and fellow long-term hackers with fundamental flaws in their own swings. George's age and his natural athletic ability helped him get the ball around the green in what golfers call "regulation." From there, his chipping and putting ability would guarantee him his share of par scores. As a result he usually won, which to George is very important. Until a few years ago, "playing for it" worked for George.

Now, the environment has changed! He moved to another city and joined a private golf club. The fairways are narrower, longer, and surrounded by long rough and thick stands of trees and brush. George is, of course, a bit more chronologically gifted: his nerves, strength, and coordination are not quite what they were when he was younger. He, too, has changed!

"Playing for it" doesn't work as well any more. He now has a whole new group of golfing buddies. They are all in his age range and most of them are not in as good shape as he is, yet they all beat him. They hit the ball farther, with more control, and with less effort. George is really frustrated and puts in even longer hours at the driving range practicing "playing for it." If he related to his golf in an R-overwhelmed (withdrawing and avoiding) manner, he would, as many under the same circumstances do, simply quit. But George is not a quitter. Instead, he copes by working harder at his maladaptive strategy. He is entrenched!

It is not as though he doesn't know what to do. He has taken some lessons and his club professional has told him he needs to swing more from the inside out, turn his hips and finish on his left side, and make a longer, more fluid swing. George is in good shape and certainly has the physical ability to change his swing. The problem is that he can't do it all the time and the price he must pay for long-term improvement is short-term deterioration and unpredictability. George's fear of looking awkward or out of control, and of spending even more time in the woods and the rough, is preventing him from making the necessary adaptive changes. In a classic R-entrenched pattern, he knows what to do, but his lack of comfort with change holds him back. The basic hazard of the entrenched also looms over his head: giving up, sinking down into the overwhelmed category, and withdrawing from the fray. In George's situation, this would involve becoming overcome by his frustration over "playing for it," dropping out of the club, and quitting the game.

George's golfing adventures illustrate three points in regard to the R-entrenched behavior pattern:

- *When our environment changes and we need to do things differently, our most natural response is to work harder at the way we did things before the change.* We need to go against the grain—work counter to our natural inclinations—because our equivalent of continuing to play for it is not a good strategy for our own growth and development or for the productivity and survival of our organizations.

- *Entrenched employees do useful work, but their fear of change puts severe limits on their productivity and contribution.* This in turn has a negative impact on their self-esteem. Playing for it when surrounded by others who have learned to do things more efficiently and with more zest is not self-affirming. Spending time in the long rough or behind trees and bushes when we know how to do it better is not a happy way to play a game or spend a career.

- *Having the ability to change and knowing how to change does not equate to making it happen!* In George's case, his need for predictability and control and his concern for not looking even more inept in front of his friends holds him back. Learning new, more adaptive behavior always involves confronting some of our long-standing demons and old tapes. Looking silly or stupid, losing control, or losing face are powerful forces that can keep us trapped in the upper left box.

The Metaphor of the Rings

The story of the rings is an oft-told metaphor among certain applied behavioral scientists. It begins with the vision of a series of gymnastic rings, hanging by ropes. A person jumps from a platform and grabs a ring with the right hand, then—while maintaining momentum—reaches out and grabs the next ring with the left hand; then, again, grasps the next ring with the right, keeping the rhythm and moving through the line of rings.

The learning points of this story are that you have to let go of one ring before you can grab hold of another, and there comes a moment of truth when, if you want to continue to move, you have neither hand on a ring, but must have faith that you will have the ability to grasp the ring in front of you! Another version is that in moments of severe change and flux you are moving through the rings blindfolded, and need to have faith that there will be a ring in front of you when you let go of the old one.

Hanging Around with the Overwhelmed

Returning to the overwhelmed for a moment, the metaphor is useful for that category as well. One way to conceptualize the plight of an overwhelmed ring traveler is that the person freezes and does not let go of a ring. This, of course, stops the momentum and leaves the next ring out of reach. The victim is literally left hanging, going nowhere and growing weaker and weaker. Unless someone gives a hand, literally frees up a hand by swinging the next ring closer, the overwhelmed ring traveler will eventually let go and drop to the floor. In the case of the overwhelmed, this assistance comes in the form of symptom relief.

The Perilous Journey of the Entrenched

This is the story of one person's travels through the rings. It can be applied to many others. This person had spent many years perfecting traveling down a seemingly endless and very predictable row of rings. The rings were of equal spacing and size and stretched over the horizon. He was a very good ring swinger and was very happy. He was able to move swiftly, efficiently, and predictably along his narrow corridor of interchangeable rings. His plans were to keep swinging until retirement.

One morning he jumped from the platform, beginning another day's journey. From the time he hit the first ring it was apparent that things had changed! The first ring was a bit off to the side. The next was slightly closer than he was used to. As he continued to move he discovered that the new ring world was, indeed, very different— the rings were spaced at unpredictable distances, some closer together, others farther apart. To make matters worse, the height began to vary! He had to struggle to reach some that were high, and drop down to catch some below him. Then they grew very slippery, as though someone had put oil on them. As if that were not enough, they began to vary in size, and then he discovered a few that were not rings at all but trapeze bars—some of them broken and hanging only by a single chain on one side. Then there was the light—it would suddenly grow very dark or the lights would become glaringly bright. There was no pattern and it was very disorienting.

He then discovered two distinct varieties of fellow travelers. For the first time in his swinging career, people began to pass him, traveling with an ease and grace that seemed impossible on that confusing and unpredictable array of gymnastic apparatus and rapidly changing visibility. They were moving much faster than he was willing to risk, although, after watching them, he thought he could learn how to do it. He next found a second type of fellow traveler. Only the people in this group were not moving—they were stationary—

hanging from individual rings or trapezes with both hands. They got in his way and he really needed to be agile to duck around them.

There was no relief. Things kept getting more difficult and he grew tired, angry, and frustrated. Why couldn't things be what they were. He had really excelled at swinging through predictable, evenly spaced rings. Maybe he should just stop and take a break. He was so tired and it was so difficult trying to move through the new rings using his old skills. Perhaps he could take a quick rest on the next one, just hold on with both hands for a while. . . .

The Entrenched: Four Dimensions

As was the case with the overwhelmed, what follows is an overview of four perspectives of the R-entrenched: how they feel, how they typically react to transitions, their learning behavior, and what they need to be successful survivors. Again, I will include some typical descriptions.

How Entrenched Employees Feel

Anxious, frustrated, and angry. Since entrenched employees know how to change but are unable to do it, they are very frustrated. They experience anxiety because they know they are not adjusting to the new environment and are concerned about their security. They are angry because the environment has changed and they want it to remain the same. Typical descriptions of these feelings are:

> "He lashed out at me last week about the change in the customer order system. It isn't my fault that he won't take the time to learn how to use it!"

> "She is really worried about losing her job, but if she keeps doing things the same old way she is going to ensure that is exactly what happens."

"I understand how he feels. Believe me, I've been there, but you have to move on. You can't live in the past—and things have changed."

Threatened by a sudden change in previously valued behavior. Entrenched employees are ego-involved with past patterns of behavior and organizational identity. Who they are is where they work, what they do, and how they do it, so any change in the environment is a threat to their identity. Typical descriptions:

"He keeps telling me that 'we are forgetting what made us who we are.' He really takes the change personally."

"She fights all the changes."

"He is the best corporate historian going. I haven't got time to listen to all his old war stories."

Unrealistically confident that past skills are still valid. Entrenched employees can not let go of old competencies and priorities even though new goals and approaches will facilitate their own contribution and the organization's productivity. Typical descriptions:

"Cycle time means nothing to that group. They are developing products the way we did it before deregulation."

"No one cares about those accounting reports. They look nice, but they could save lots of time if they just threw them away."

"She can't keep dealing with customers the way we used to do it. They have a lot more choices now."

Guilty over surviving when others left. The entrenched are the primary carriers of survivor guilt. Overwhelmed employees are too self-absorbed to experience the feeling, BSers are incapable of feeling guilt, and learners have found ways to deal with it. Entrenched employees react to transitions by doing business as usual. Since others with the exact same behavior and coping style have become lay-off victims, entrenched survivors are set up to experience survivor sickness. Typical descriptions:

> "Everyone in my department wonders how they were lucky enough to stay. I can't see any difference between us and the ones who were let go."

> "No wonder he feels bad. The whole department is a drain on our bottom line. None of them are helping us turn things around. I don't know why any of them are still here."

Reluctant to take risks. Those who exhibit R-entrenched behavior are risk averse. Since they are locked into narrow and previously successful behaviors, they cannot get outside the box to experiment with new behaviors or take creative risks. They are trapped in their old coping patterns. Typical descriptions:

> "You are not going to change him. He is going to do it the old way until he dies."

> "She bombed out of the transition team. She couldn't break set. She slowed us down and I'm glad she is gone."

Unhappy but unwilling to start over in the external job market. Entrenched employees are not only entrenched in old patterns of behavior, they are entrenched within the organization. They are terrified of change and therefore hold on to their jobs with a death grip. They will stay until you pry them out. Typical descriptions:

> "He needs to go, but he's afraid he would not fit in any other organization."

> "I asked him if he was so damn unhappy, why he didn't update his résumé? I know he won't do it."

"She has some marketable skills, but she has no confidence anyone will hire her."

How Entrenched Employees React to Transitions

Blame and complain. Entrenched employees are heavily psycholog-
ically invested in the past. They want things to return to normal
and their frustration with transition and change is manifested in
their need to find scapegoats. Typical descriptions:

> "She blames me for the new production schedule. I'm just trying
> to get all the gears to mesh here. She knows we have to go
> faster and it would help us all if she would stop making it per-
> sonal with everyone."

> "He sure has a long bitch list! That kind of conversation gets
> old fast."

> "If you listen to her, it's the bosses' fault, it's the union's fault,
> we're in trouble because 'they' don't have a strategy!"

Acknowledge the need for change, but resist changing. Those who
live in the upper left box are there because they have the ability to
change, but, because they are unable to let go of the past, they
have great difficulty making it happen for themselves. There is
often a wide gap between what they say and what they do. Typical
descriptions:

> "As a top manager, he sure talks a good ball game. If I hear him
> talk about empowerment again, I'm going to throw up. He
> tells everyone about empowerment and power-up, and all he
> does is tighten the screws every time we get bad news."

> "I got her to look at us as internal customers, but I had to drag
> her into it."

> "He asks me for feedback and when I give it to him, he blows
> it off!"

Work harder than ever at previously successful behavior. This is a classic coping mechanism for those exhibiting R-entrenched behavior. A core strategy for many entrenched employees, misguided though it may be, involves working their way back to the good old days. The deeply entrenched will often engage in an action frenzy, working very long and very hard on the wrong things. Not only do they focus on the wrong objectives, they approach this misguided activity using behavior patterns that don't fit the new reality. Typical descriptions:

> "His knee-jerk reaction to the integration problem was to establish a task force. Not only is a task force the wrong way to handle this issue, but, true to form, he has loaded it with his old cronies who haven't had a fresh idea in years. It's the blind leading the blind."

> "He is driving us all mad. He has given us an impossible deadline to write a whole series of new processes. We are all working too hard on the wrong problem. We don't need new processes, we need new technology. If he wasn't driving himself and us so hard he would see that—or we might be able to get him to listen."

Try to ride it out until things return to normal. This is a similar reaction to that of the overwhelmed employees. Except that the overwhelmed have a vague hope that things might get better, while those who are entrenched have a fervent desire—and often really believe—that the clock can be turned back. Typical descriptions:

> "We had this really weird staff meeting. She actually told us to have patience, keep plugging, and things would take care of themselves. I can't believe she really said that!"

> "I need to help them get it through their thick heads that we have been acquired. That changes everything. They can't keep

relying on their past assumptions about the way things are and should be. The truth is they aren't and won't be."

"He thinks if he keeps his head down and works hard he can keep his job. I hope it works for him, but I'm not optimistic."

How Entrenched Employees Operate as Learners

Narrow and restricted learning strategy based on the past. The major learning strategy of R-entrenched employees is to tenaciously hold on to tactics that have served them well in the past. This rigid adherence to the past has the effect of blocking the essential experimentation and risk taking that leads to the personal change and growth necessary to contribute in the new reality. Typical descriptions:

> "We can't stand it anymore! He's doing what we did ten years ago when we had a protected market. He has got to make a decision and go with it."

> "The silos are gone. She can't operate in isolation and needs to learn to include others and seek their input even if they are in different departments. She really needs to start doing that."

> "He is not going to make it here unless he changes his conservative, risk-avoiding style. That is not the new culture and he is out of step."

Unconsciously block out the need for change. Because entrenched employees have a deep psychological attachment to the past, they often have a strategy of waiting it out, anticipating that things will eventually return to normal. Given this strategy as an underpinning, the need for change is, at one level, seen as irrelevant and, at a much deeper level, is experienced as very threatening. It is a threat that is often buried in the unconscious and it results in a blockage of the basic need to make any change at all. Typical descriptions:

"He refuses to understand the problem."

"She and her department are trying to ride it out. They haven't changed one thing since the merger."

"He really believes that this is a short-term blip and if we just suck it in, there will be a turnaround."

Equate action frenzy with contribution and activity with learning. At first glance, this appears similar to the overwhelmed response of equating activity with learning. There are, however, basic differences. The overwhelmed spend a lot of their time attempting to look busy, but because of their withdrawal and avoidance it is just an act. Entrenched employees really are busy! Like George and his golfing slice, they work harder and harder at perfecting their maladaptive behavior. This can come across to the rest of the organization as a mad frenzy of activity, particularly if the R-entrenched behavior is emanating from a manager with control over resources. Typical descriptions:

"She sure generates a lot of paper. The tougher things get, the more memos she writes."

"I'm glad I got out of that department. They work late every night . . . work weekends. They have more projects, meetings, reports, and task forces than exist in the whole division . . . and it's all smoke and mirrors. It is all going to explode one of these days."

"He thinks he's helping turn the place around. He is just working harder at the same old stuff and, unfortunately, he's getting in the way of some of his people who really do know what is needed."

What Entrenched Employees Need to Be Successful Survivors

Understanding and help in coping with guilt, anger, and frustration. The core issue with those trapped in the upper left box of the R-entrenched is their death grip on the past. This manifests itself in some debilitating symptoms that need to be dealt with before they can move on toward greater personal growth and organizational contribution. The first priority is symptom relief. They, too, need level-two work. Their symptoms are different from those of the overwhelmed. Entrenched employees have more guilt, anger, and frustration—and they are more vocal about it. A grieving session with a roomful of entrenched employees is much louder and hotter than the quiet, sad atmosphere of a group of the overwhelmed. Ideas for intervention:

- Facilitated venting sessions, designed to get the anger, guilt, and frustration out on the table.
- Activities such as task forces, meetings, and work teams where entrenched employees can connect with those who are succeeding by using new, more relevant behavior patterns.
- Counseling, feedback, and coaching sessions with internal or external resources who are not in the direct management chain and who can encourage grieving and provide feedback and coaching. These outside sessions work particularly well with senior management.

Feedback, encouragement, and support. Those who are entrenched respond well to a certain type of coaching. Not the Vince Lombardi variety—uninhibited pep talks and tirades will just cause them to put up more barriers and become more deeply entrenched. What is needed is a combination of therapist Carl Rogers's (1961) strategy of unconditional positive regard, and the gentle but persistent nudging of a mother bird pushing her brood from the nest and into the sky. The entrenched can be coached out of their box and toward the community of learners. However, if the coaching is done in a heavy-handed or callous manner, they will either become more deeply entrenched or drop down into the world of the overwhelmed. Ideas for intervention:

- Straight performance feedback by a competent boss. This feedback should clearly and in a nonthreatening manner articulate the specific new behavior that is needed. It should be followed up with assignments that provide the opportunity to practice new behaviors while receiving feedback and coaching.

• Load experiences for success. Find situations where the entrenched employee can, without fear of ridicule or failure, try out new behavior. Task forces, self-directed work teams, and supportive colleagues can really help. It is important that these groups be made up of learners who embrace the new culture—people who will automatically want to help. The groups should not be made up of the overwhelmed, entrenched, or BS types, or more will be lost than gained.

• Transfer high-potential entrenched employees into developmentally optimistic environments. This can be a permanent or a temporary situation. There is nothing that will break down the walls of the entrenched fortress more than sustained interaction with a group of creative, learning optimists, or than working for a boss who is a true learner.

Phased-in transitions with a bridge from the old to the new. The entrenched can't get from their current reality to the new culture without some kind of a safe connection. They need help to build on their old skills and transport them to the new culture. They also need connections back to their old entrenched world in case they need to retreat. You can't just give entrenched employees a one-way ticket to the new reality: they need the comfort of a return ticket in case the new reality becomes too frightening. Ideas for intervention:

• Find a use for their old skills in the new world. If a manager has an internal focus and spends most of his time in analytical activities that are no longer needed, put him with a customer or someone close to customers and have him analyze a client's problem. A creative leader can always find a developmental way to apply the old skills to the new world. It may be a shotgun wedding at first but the name of the game is to craft developmental assignments. I have seen many of these assignments deliver payoffs that far exceeded everyone's expectations.

• Maintain some of the old structure and cultural artifacts. Departments can radically change their work content, but their names and physical locations don't have to change. One organization dissolved their corporate traffic department and the person who had managed that function became part of the accounting department, where he analyzed travel costs. For nearly eighteen months, however, they let him keep his title and his old office. There was a little inconvenience and it wasn't a neat fit on the organization chart, but keeping the bridge to the old world was a very powerful factor in this entrenched manager's successful transition. Titles, ritualistic meetings, committee assignments, and membership in external professional associations are all bridges back to the old world. If the cost isn't prohibitive, and the entrenched employee has potential, it makes no sense to burn these bridges prematurely.

• Craft a series of success-loaded mini challenges, as recommended for overwhelmed employees. The objective for the overwhelmed is to pull them out of the mire of withdrawal and get them connected to work. The objective for the entrenched is much more focused. It involves testing out new behavior in environments where there is a strong probability of success. The crafting of these experiences is a labor-intensive and somewhat artificial process. The effort is worthwhile, however, if you have a high-potential entrenched employee whose contribution to the organization you want to maximize.

• Use simulation training. In general, skills training will be rejected by those exhibiting R-entrenched behavior. What works extremely well, however, is participation in simulations. There are a number of behavioral simulations on the market, and a few are very powerful. In these simulations, the entrenched employee can practice new behavior in a safe place and get developmental feedback on old behavior patterns that do not fit the new environment.

How Many Rocks in Your Pack?

A key strategy for helping both the overwhelmed and the entrenched involves facilitating the emotional release provided by grieving. Some organizations don't like the word grieving and call it *venting* instead. This process is described in the pyramid intervention model (Appendix A) as a level-two intervention. These interventions are not one-time fixes, nor are they limited to overwhelmed or entrenched employees; we all need them. There are only two conditions necessary to qualify for this need to deal with accumulated organizational emotional baggage—we need to be alive, and we need to work in an organization!

In one of my first corporate jobs, I worked for an ex-marine officer. He was gung-ho and freshly out of the corps. His name was Bill and every time he gave me an assignment he would say, "I have another rock for your pack, sir!"

It took me a couple of interactions but I soon understood this statement was a carryover from a diabolical practice done to recruits in basic training. To make their marching and double-time more "interesting," the drill instructors put rocks in their backpacks.

To Bill, I had an invisible backpack and it was his job as my boss to keep giving me assignments: putting rocks in my pack. Bill really liked to impress his boss by all the work he took on. He also liked to delegate, and unfortunately, I was the only professional on his staff. He must have thought I had an incredibly large pack, because he kept piling on the rocks and some of them were real boulders!

One day I said to Bill, "Boss, my knees are buckling, my shoulders are chaffed, my back is breaking, and my feet are getting flat. If you put any more rocks in my pack, I'm going to buckle and collapse onto the deck!" By that time, I'd learned to talk like a marine.

Bill, who deep down was a caring person, surprised me when he said, "Well, let me help you lighten your load, sir!" We then proceeded to rearrange my work and he eventually hired a couple more pack carriers.

Many years have passed since I was "taking hills" with Bill. He taught me a great deal, but most of all, he gave me a set of lenses to see the invisible backpacks that we all wear. I have learned something more: the rocks that go in these packs are not tasks as Colonel Bill led me to believe—rather, they are grievances, feelings, and unresolved interpersonal issues.

This past summer, I had occasion to reflect upon the way we all put rocks in other people's packs, and our need for help in removing them. We can't get them out by ourselves. My wife and I were driving back from a vacation at the beach in South Carolina. It had not been a good week; it was extremely hot, humid, and crowded. Our accommodations were noisy, not very clean, and overpriced. We measured the days by the number of showers we took. A four-shower day meant we left the air-conditioned condominium four times. It was so humid that each time we left the building we would be dripping wet before we were a hundred yards from the door.

It is just over a six-hour drive from Hilton Head Island to our home in Greensboro. The first hour was spent in unnatural silence. Finally she said, "You did it again!"

"Did what?" I asked, knowing full well where she was heading.

"You picked a bad week and a lousy place for our vacation!"

"It's going to be a long drive," I muttered.

"And then there was New York!" she continued.

"It's going to be a very long drive," I repeated, thinking of the disastrous weekend I had organized without her involvement six months earlier.

I looked across the front seat and could see that she had an unnatural bulge in her pack. She had picked up some interpersonal rocks during the last half year, and I could tell she was feeling the weight.

My wife, Diana, and I have a very good marriage and—after thirty-something years—we have worked most things out. We do have the lingering issue of her need to participate in decisions that affect both of us, and my proclivity to make them on my own. As marital issues go, this is not in the major league, but what was important that hot morning was our joint need to work on reducing the bulge in her pack. The danger of unattended packs is that they either get too heavy and wear down the bearer, or the pebble effect becomes operational and the pack carrier takes it off and beats the person who deposited the pebble over the head with the pack.

The pebble effect is the interpersonal backpack equivalent of the story of the straw that broke the camel's back. The person who puts in the pebble that causes the burden to be too severe is the surprised recipient of an outburst of repressed grievances and aggravations that may have resided in the pack for a very long time.

An enduring relationship is one based on the ability of each party to tend to the other's pack. Diana and I work very hard to make sure neither of our packs grow too heavy. We emptied her pack, and removed a few stones I didn't realize I was carrying before we hit the North Carolina border. The rest of the drive was the best part of that vacation.

Central to our human condition are our feelings and emotions. They give us our highs and they give us our lows. As we interact with others, we experience joy, love, and humor. We also encounter our fair share of the not-so-pleasant emotions: anger, hurt, and bitterness. Unless dealt with immediately, these are stored in our packs to be processed at a later time. It's the "pay me now, or pay me later" situation. Under normal circumstances, people with reasonable insight and interpersonal skills are able to keep their packs relatively light. The way this is done is through inter-action with others, verbalizing feelings, and processing them with other people. If we allow our packs to get too heavy, bad things happen. We get physically or mentally ill, we grow cynical, we surprise others—and often ourselves—by lashing out because of the pebble effect.

Unlike the Old West, where people had to check their guns before they could enter certain towns, we don't drop our packs at the door of the office—we bring them to work with us. In times of transition, downsizing, and restructuring, organizations drop some heavy rocks in our packs. We differ in our ability to lighten our load. Those with overwhelmed and entrenched response patterns have a particularly difficult time. The rocks they must bear are called anger, fear, guilt, depression, and anxiety—and they are exceptionally heavy!

In many organizations, a significant percentage of the surviving workforce is made up of employees with R-overwhelmed and R-entrenched behavior patterns. Unless means are provided to lighten their load, they will spend their work life staggering around, wobbly kneed and reeling. This is not a workforce equipped to compete in a global environment, nor one able to implement a culture change. That is why level-two work is so important. It helps lighten the load and makes it easier for employees to help themselves and their organizations. If organizations want lean, aggressive, market-driven employees, they can't send them out to compete on the global playing field staggering under the weight of an unrelieved pack!

Everyone has a pack; and the accumulation of rocks is not limited to those who are overwhelmed or entrenched. The boss and the helper have special needs; they need to attend to their packs before they can be much good at helping others. Pack lightening is a communal activity. Individuals cannot empty their own packs. If we are to lead productive lives and help our organizations cope with change and transition, we need to forge organizational cultures where it is not only an acceptable practice but a required activity to engage in mutual pack lightening.

Encountering the Entrenched: Up Close and Personal

This section includes advice on how to interact with bosses and subordinates who are entrenched. It also offers tips for those readers who suspect they are behaving with an entrenched response pattern.

If You Work for One

If you report to an entrenched boss, and assuming you are not entrenched yourself, you need to do some upward managing. Entrenched bosses are not sympathetic to employees who have made a better transition. In fact, they are often angry and abusive to those who don't buy into their strategy of waiting until things return to normal. You have some options:

• Distance yourself from the boss by losing yourself in the work. If you are a learner, chances are you are in great demand and are really challenged. Spend your time on cross-functional work teams, task forces, and special projects. Minimize your interaction with your boss and bond around the work you do, not who you happen to report to.

• Connect with—and don't be afraid to use as protection—others who are as or more powerful in the organization than your boss. If you have the skills and perspective to help the organization through a difficult transition, lots of organizational leaders will want to protect you.

• Negotiate limits. Do not let your entrenched boss suck you into the action frenzy. Commit your time to those projects and activities that will really make a difference. Confronting a boss in the midst of an irrelevant action frenzy requires courage, but it is worth it. The alternative is to waste your time and collude in a trivial activity at a time when the organization really needs you to be doing important things.

• Get out if you can't make the current assignment work. If you have the right stuff to help the organization, there should be an abundance of transfer opportunities. If you can't manage a transfer, then leave the organization. Staying just is not worth it.

If One Works for You

If you have one or more entrenched employees reporting to you, you have the opportunity to do some important development. Assuming you have decided that the entrenched employee has potential and is worth your time and effort, you can do the following:

• Find or craft developmental assignments that call for new skills and have a strong probability of success.

• Send the employee to a behavioral simulation that will provide structured feedback and set some concrete behavioral goals.

- Use your coaching skills: feedback, support, confrontation, empathy. Your task is to nudge the entrenched employee out of the fortress and toward the fellowship of learners, without overdoing it and knocking someone down to the colony of the overwhelmed.

If You Are One

If you conclude through feedback or reflection that you are exhibiting R-entrenched behavior, consider the following:

- Find a way to deal with your symptoms. Chances are you are feeling frustrated and angry. There is also a strong probability that you have a case of survivor sickness. You need to lighten your pack and you need to be quick about it! If the organization will not or cannot help you, seek outside assistance. You are not going to get far while staggering under the weight of a heavy pack.

- Find safe places to practice new behavior. If you are unsure what kind of behavior is appropriate, get some feedback from someone inside the organization. Find a person who is making a good personal adjustment and who respects you enough to tell you the truth. You may want to test this new behavior outside your primary organization, in volunteer or community groups. Another excellent opportunity to practice new behavior and to get solid feedback is in a behavioral simulation. If your organization has an internal program, sign up; if they are willing to send you to an outside experience, all the better.

- Try not to feel bad about your residence in the upper left box. It is a better location than the box directly below you. Your task is to find ways to venture out and experiment with new behavior. Stay out longer each day, and it won't be long before you won't have to return.

The Entrenched: Perspective and Observations

The primary task of those exhibiting R-entrenched behavior is to find ways to let go of the comfortable old and learn skills and behaviors relevant to the new reality. Helping with these efforts is time consuming and requires creativity. In most cases, it is well worth the effort. The entrenched are good, dedicated employees who are, in their way, attempting to help the organization grow and prosper. They are often performing tasks that are of value to the organization and—with some pack lightening and proper coaching—are capable of major performance improvements.

The entrenched are a large group. Many organizations estimate that the number of entrenched employees range from 30 to over 60 percent of their workforces. They are found in even greater numbers in industries such as the regional phone companies and the public utilities. R-entrenched behavior also seems to cluster around survivors from staff groups who have been heavily invested in control and rules administration. The human resource function is split. In some organizations, there are a very large number of entrenched employees; in others there are, when compared to the rest of the workforce, a disproportionate number of learners.

Organizational leaders have cause to be developmentally optimistic. Entrenched employees have the ability to change but need help with their comfort and readiness. They are already halfway toward responding to the new reality with the creativity and learning behavior that will maximize their own potential and assure a robust and viable future for the organization. Working to help the entrenched discard their old behavior patterns and facilitating their movement toward the exciting world of the true learner is a high-leverage intervention.

4

The BSer

In the lower right box of the R-factor model there resides that interesting and odoriferous character we call the BSer. We fervently sought a more scientific (if not a more politically correct) term for this type but—based on input from colleagues, clients, and personal experience—could not discover a more descriptive label. We mean BSer in its common colloquial and fetid sense. Just as the farmer distributes it on his fields, the BSer spreads it on himself and others. Those practicing R-BS behavior are con artists and the first people they fool are themselves.

Their most visible distinguishing characteristic is shown on the horizontal axis. They have a high comfort with change and this is what others see and at least initially admire. What others do not see, and a blind spot for BSers, is their inability to learn more relevant and appropriate behavior patterns—they score low on the vertical axis, capacity for change. While the entrenched know what to do (high capacity for change) but have an extremely difficult time making it happen (low comfort with change), the BSers have no problem making something—often anything—happen (high comfort) but have no idea how to learn or any desire to change (low capacity).

As illustrated in Figure 4.1, the major response pattern of the BSer involves a form of hipshooting aggressiveness. Their comfort with change and lack of any need or desire to anchor that change

Figure 4.1. The BSer: High Comfort with Change, Low Capacity for Change.

The BSer

"Makes It Up"
High Drive but
Low Substance

in new learning or behavior causes them to press for action and activity without any grounding in theory or understanding. A key descriptor for the R-BS behavior pattern is "high drive and low substance."

We and our clients estimate that from 10 to 15 percent of the workforce is made up of employees evidencing the R-BS behavior pattern. This is only an estimate and it is difficult to generalize as we don't have empirical data. We also have seen what appear to be variances by industry, profession, and management level. There seem to be a large number of BSers in the entertainment industry. They are found in abundance in organizations with strong old-style marketing cultures emphasizing faith, ritual, and enthusiasm without data, analysis, or feedback. We have also found significant numbers in many political systems and a few religious organizations.

Although BSers are found at all levels in organizations, they tend to cluster in upper middle management and in lower upper management. If they get too low in the hierarchy, the sheer volume of work renders their style ineffective. If they venture too high up the management pyramid, their lack of substance becomes readily visible. There is nowhere to hide and those who have risen to the top of organizations are very perceptive and can readily sniff out the odor of BS when it begins to pollute the rarefied air of top management.

No-Toes Rides Again

They called him No-Toes. He was a big-time gunslinger from the West and he shot people, he took them out, he terminated them! He was one tough dude, a cold loner who was paid well for his trade.

Jerry, the no-toed gunslinger's real name, didn't ride in narrow eyed and squinting at the rising sun on a stallion with flared nostrils and a sheen of sweat. He arrived calmly, with no dust or perspiration, wearing a three-piece suit and ensconced in an aisle seat in the first-class section of a 747. Appearances are deceptive; he, in his way, was just as deadly as the gunslingers from the Old West.

Language patterns offer insight to the unconscious. It is not accidental that the language of layoffs features words such as terminate, take out, shoot, and kill. This is the language of assassination and, at one level, this was Jerry's business. Rather than bullets, his guns were loaded with pink slips. By education, Jerry was an accountant, by profession a banker, by behavior a gunslinger, and by R-type a BSer!

No-Toes had made a career out of moving into organizations that were in trouble, quickly making decisions, and stimulating action. They were often the wrong decisions and the action frequently moved the organization in the wrong direction, but in the kind of paralyzed organizations that hired him, a quick, dogmatic, and prescriptive decision was generally more valued than one that was deliberative and participative. These kinds of overwhelmed organizations were looking for an answer, and Jerry was a solution looking for a problem.

Like most practitioners of R-BS behavior, Jerry was gifted at making quick, clear, and persuasively articulated decisions. The problem was—as with his fellow residents of the lower right corner—one of information flow. It travels directly from the ears to the mouth with no interruption for processing in the brain! Since BSers are compelled to articulate and sell any direction or decision regardless of substance, they are very dangerous. They are capable of taking the overwhelmed individual or the overwhelmed organization in the wrong direction with a speed and intensity that can move them to a point of no return.

All of No-Toes's past turnarounds, reengineering feats, and restructurings had only one basic tactic—the reduction of a large percentage of the workforce. The Midwest financial service organization that hired Jerry and flew him in from the West Coast suffered the same fate. They really did need to do something with their staff—but they needed a lot more. They had too many people with the wrong skills and no coherent strategy. No-Toes cured the symptom but not the disease. After the people left there was still no strategy and many of the ones who left had the very skills the organization needed to pull off a turnaround. Jerry cut too deeply, cut the wrong people, and did nothing for the survivors. After a wild and tempestuous first year, the gunslinger had created an overwhelmed, risk-averse, nonproductive workforce, who, even if they could shake off the ravages of layoff survivor sickness, would need a massive injection of skills training to move the organization forward.

In style, Jerry took the missequenced process of ready—fire—aim to a new level. He was such an aggressive hipshooter that he was described by his colleagues as pulling the trigger before he even got the gun out of the holster—thus blowing off his toes. It wasn't long before No-Toes himself was forced out of the organization, unfortunately landing a similar gunslinging role in still another overwhelmed organization. Despite some last-minute heroic efforts by a few courageous survivors, the organization that No-Toes rode into town to save didn't make it! What remains of that once proud and independent bank is a very small part of a much larger financial services organization. The gunslinger rode in from the West to save the town and the result was that the town was downsized, reengineered, and annexed by a larger municipality.

No-Toes's wild ride through this previously sleepy but independent financial services organization demonstrates three points in regard to the R-BS type:

- They can, because of their drive to positively frame and persuasively sell any direction or action, lead the overwhelmed—individuals and organizations alike—in the wrong direction. They frequently get everyone involved into even deeper and hotter water.

- They should not be empowered! Because of their high drive, low substance, and compulsion to take action, they are very dangerous in power roles.

- They are very seductive. At a time when calm deliberation, objective analysis, and learning are necessary, organizations—particularly those that are overwhelmed—perceive a paradoxical need for a clear direction. They want someone to give them an easy answer; to show them the way. Organizations and individuals need to spend the necessary regenerative time in the neutral zone. The essential learning does not come from the outside and will not happen if the process is rushed. The siren song of the BSer is very compelling to overwhelmed individuals and organizations seeking external fixes to problems that require internal learning.

Feedback and the BSer

The concept of 360-degree management feedback involves an employee's self-assessment, usually on a testlike series of rating scales dealing with a number of factors that describe on-the-job behavior. The employee's boss, peers, and direct reports also complete instruments measuring their perceptions of the same factors. Managers getting this feedback can thus compare the way they see themselves with the views of those beside, above, and below them on the organizational chart.

Those exhibiting R-BS behavior have a hard time accepting any feedback and the 360-degree variety is no easier to take. It, however, provides an interesting set of lenses through which to understand their behavior and the differing perceptions of peers, bosses, and employees. BSers, in times of change and stress, can in the short term manage to fool their bosses. Their self-ratings and those of their bosses are often only slightly dissimilar. They have a harder time with their peers and, if the organization requires a high degree of cross-functional interaction, there are frequently marked differences at this level—with the BSer's self-rating higher than the peer ratings. There are almost always large and significant differences when you look down the hierarchy, with the employees of a BSer consistently rating the boss lower than the boss does.

While not all those with gaps between self and subordinate ratings are BSers, there is another clue. True BSers will blow off and attempt to explain away the data. They will tell you that the employees are wrong, they are troublemakers, they are too new to have an accurate reading, they don't understand the true nature or pressures of the job. The BSer will find a number of creative ways to deny the data.

The Finger Pointing Index

My colleague Kerry Bunker points out another distinguishing characteristic of the BSer. When attempting to argue with and deny feedback, a number of them tend to wave an index finger in your face while talking. He tells of when, in a moment of frustration, he grabbed the BSer's waving right index finger with his own left hand.

"Let's see if we can have a meaningful conversation for five minutes without your waving your finger in my face!" said Kerry, still holding on.

After a couple of strained moments, the BSer said, "Kerry, I think I'm having a powerful learning experience."

"That's great! Describe it," answered Kerry, still hanging on to the finger but feeling good about his intervention.

"I'm learning that I'm going to deck you if you don't let go of my finger!" shouted the BSer with a fierce look in his eye and a balled up left fist.

Kerry let go of the finger both because he couldn't have held on much longer and he truly thought he might get hit. He has, however, extracted everlasting revenge—he selected the original version of the finger-pointing character in Figure 4.1!

The BS Response: Four Dimensions

This section presents a four-dimensional perspective of the R-BSers: their feelings, their typical reactions to transitions, their learning behavior, and what they need to survive organizational trauma and transition.

How BSers Feel

Comfortable with the need for change. Those who reside in the lower right box of the R-factor model are there in part because the prospect of change and transition does not faze them. They respond to organizational trauma in the same manner that the fictional Alfred E. Newman of *MAD Magazine* fame responded to all of life's trials: with a toothy grin and his classic motto, "What, me worry?" (Tuleja, 1994).

The reason those reacting to change and transition with the BS response remain in their corner is that their comfort with change is not matched by their ability to learn and adapt new and more relevant coping strategies. Alfred E. Newman has been grinning and not worrying through the trauma of the sixties, the anguish of Vietnam, the betrayal of Watergate, and the unanticipated collapse of the Soviet Union. He is an interesting but increasingly irrelevant guy. Who would really want to follow him? We want our leaders to change and be changed by events. We want them to worry! We want them to learn how to make things better. Typical descriptions of BSers' reactions to change:

> "None of this seems to bother him. I can't believe he is so optimistic . . . does he understand what is going on?"

> "That group is driving a car at sixty miles per hour and heading for a brick wall. They don't even have their seat belts on and they are passing around a bottle of champagne, celebrating."

> "He has never been happier . . . only problem is he's taking us south when we should go north and west when we should go east."

Ready to take action—compelled to do something, anything. The primary response pattern of the BSer involves taking action, frequently engaging in an aggressive, hipshooting response to change. Because of the BSer's lack of concern with learning, this action taking occurs unfettered by strategy, theory, analysis, or new behavioral patterns. Typical descriptions:

> "She reorganized the entire department with about ten minutes thought and no consultation with those of us doing the work. Nothing has changed . . . that's the way she always reacts to problems. We don't tell her she has not fixed a damn thing."

> "The plan is to outsource and decentralize. At least that's what we think he said. We are moving too fast . . . we ought to at least find out what the rest of the division is doing."

> "He is pacing his office like a caged tiger. He wants to do something. I hope he waits until we understand the problem!"

Frustrated with the confusion and whining. Because of their comfort with change, compulsion to act, and difficulty with learning,

BSers are surprised by, and unsympathetic to, the pain and stress felt by others. Typical descriptions:

> "He wants me to tell them, 'quit bitching and get on with it!' He just doesn't understand the real agony that is going on down there."

> "It is going to be a hard sell with her. She doesn't think we need grieving or venting sessions."

> "His response to this post-merger mess was to write a memo to all employees in the plant. It came off demeaning and punishing . . . he even attached a vision statement. That's all we need now, another nicely worded vision statement. That will not help us straighten things out."

Confident in ability to function in any situation. BSers not only con others, they con themselves. Those with the BS response have faith that they can handle any crisis with aggressive hipshooting. Typical descriptions:

> "If we could turn her bluster into profits we would be out of the woods."

> "I don't think he has a clue what the real issues are. He just doesn't know he doesn't know."

How BSers React to Transitions

Jockey for positions of influence. Times of transition and trauma present opportunities for those who have comfort with change and are not held back by the need to learn and understand. Their misguided optimism and ability to provide a quick sense of direction can result in promotion to positions of influence. This has two bad results: it gives them the power to lead the organization the wrong direction, and it pushes aside more deliberative and less aggressive leaders who are seeking long-term solutions. Typical descriptions:

"He never should have been put into that job. There are at least ten others who could have helped us get at the real issues."

"We hired another guy from outside. That is really demoralizing for those of us who have been waiting our turn. I guess they don't think we are tough enough, but how would they know?"

"There are about a dozen hotshots with 'the answer,' floating around here. I hope the people upstairs don't listen to them . . . we are not going to get there with a quick fix."

Press for quick solutions and decisive action. The BSers' only reaction to transition is to *do* something. This is because they lack the orientation to *think* something or *learn* something. The outgrowth of a single option is a compulsion to act. It is the only way for BSers to validate their existence. It is a perversion of Descartes. The BSer acts, therefore, he is! Typical descriptions:

"We decided more in that meeting than we have in the last six months. I hope he's right but my gut tells me we are moving way too fast."

"She is really pushing to do something big and splashy. I think we need to take some small steps first."

May initially come across as a beacon in the darkness; but ultimately become transparent. The BSers' clarity, direction, and aggressive decision making are initially valued during times of transition. With time, however, the lack of substance becomes more apparent. Typical descriptions:

"He came on like gang busters, but the Board got wise to him after a year. He spent a lot of money and left us in worse shape than he found us. That isn't much of a legacy!"

"I started out really liking to work for her . . . now, I do it all on my own. She is no help at all, no value-added."

"He gave us a sense of direction but it was the wrong direction."

Often fool superiors. Those who respond to transitions with R-BS behavior are frequently able to convince their superiors they are doing meaningful work. While most bosses ultimately find them out, BSers seem to be able to keep them in the dark for long periods of time. This is both because organizational leaders are distracted by their own issues, and because the action orientation of the BSer is reassuring to a stressed and overcommitted boss. Typical descriptions:

"He kept leading us further and further down the path. I don't know why they didn't stop him. Everyone here knew."

"He has a blind spot. I would fire that guy in a minute . . . doesn't he see what is happening?"

"When they finally tossed him out he got a good severance package and we aren't really jealous of that. We just wonder why it took them so long to get him out of here in the first place. He did a lot of damage and they wouldn't have had to ask many of us to find out he was a disaster."

How BSers Operate as Learners

Oblivious to core challenges. The BSers are blocked learners. They are unwilling to invest the required energy in learning new behaviors, values, and processes. Unlike the overwhelmed and the entrenched, they are comfortable living in the new reality. They, however, exist there blind to the need for a more relevant and personally satisfying way of living and contributing. Without opening themselves up to the pain and frustration of the necessary learning, their experience in the new reality is similar to that of someone residing in a foreign country with a very different culture without the ability to speak the language. They can exist, but are unable to unlock the culture or make a useful contribution. Typical descriptions:

> "She doesn't understand what it will take to get this place started again."

> "We are not going to be able to sell our way into the future . . . we need some new products and a new strategy. I wish he would spend some time on that and back off of the same old stuff."

> "We need some of that 'fundamental, transformational change' you are always talking about. How are we going to sell that to a management team that doesn't get it?"

Overestimate strengths; don't see weaknesses. Not only are BSers blind to the core organizational challenges, they do not see the basic drawback—the need to develop the capacity to learn how to learn. This fundamental weakness is subordinated and eclipsed by the clarity with which BSers see their ability to provide direction and take action. This imbalance results in an overuse of strengths and a blindness to the core development need. Typical descriptions:

> "He needs to take the time to learn what we are up against."

> "There is more to her role than speeches and 'sizzle.' It is important for her to learn our business . . . and our problems . . . and she doesn't seem to want to do that."

> "He is all show; no dough."

Dangerous as a risk taker. BSers should not be empowered. Their comfort with action and inability to understand the core issues almost guarantees a fast trip in the wrong direction. Unfortunately, BSers are often perceived as focused leaders and direction setters in the early stages of transitions, so they are often given too much latitude. Typical descriptions:

> "I bailed out of that department before she took me down with her. It's only a matter of time."

> "If we had too many more like him, we would be bankrupt by the end of the quarter."

> "I always thought it went, 'high risk; high reward.' She plays it differently . . . high risk, low reward . . . it's crazy!"

False prophet to the overwhelmed. The overwhelmed are desperately seeking a sense of direction and a strong person to bail them out. The BSer is only too happy to accommodate them. Typical descriptions:

> "One of Mussolini's claims to fame was that he got the trains running on time—and look what happened to him. Lots of people think he has our trains running on time. Let me tell you they're going to be disappointed. We are not in the railroad business!"

> "She has her disciples, but I am not one of them. She is taking them down the tube."

What BSers Need to Be Successful Survivors

Close supervision and careful monitoring. Those residing in the lower right corner need supervision. Organizations can not afford to turn them loose at a time of change and transition. They need to be overmanaged and underled! The boundaries of their influence and specific outcome goals need to be explicit. Ideas for intervention:

• The tried and true idea of management by objectives, with careful attention and mutual agreement as to the how of objective achievement, helps structure and control the BSer.

- Feedback systems and performance appraisals that take into account the perspective of more than just the boss. Useful tools include 360-degree feedback instruments and group performance appraisal processes.

- Concrete, measurable, and quantifiable goals. Goals need to be articulated in ways that do not leave room for the BSer's natural propensity to freelance and hipshoot.

Project and individual assignments, not line management. Organizational leaders need to resist the temptation to take false hope from the BSers' false optimism and short-sighted direction setting. Putting them in autonomous line management positions or roles where they have power and influence over a lot of people is hazardous to the health of the organization. Ideas for intervention:

- Find roles where BSers can provide value by focusing on their technical or functional specialty and combine these assignments with very clear, concrete, and measurable outcomes.

- Connect BSers with customers and take advantage of their action orientation and their optimism. Although BSers do not wear well internally, they frequently do their very best work with clients. These assignments need to be carefully crafted and limits need to be set, but a BSer, if held accountable for solving a short-term customer problem and given clear boundaries in regard to commitments and options, can often be helpful to the customer.

Developmental assignments that are safe for the organization and push the employee. Although I am normally developmentally optimistic, there is a fundamental choice that must be made. Is the developmental pain worth the potential performance gain? BSers are toxic to the organization, and unless they have high potential and can make some progress on learning new behavior, they should leave. It has been my unfortunate experience that hard-core BSers are very difficult to change. There is, however, a type of BSer that Amy Webb (in a personal, written communication, 1996) refers to as an *uninformed optimist.* She writes: "The uninformed optimist is eager, ready for action, but out of touch with what is going on around him.

Real understanding is not cultivated—it takes time, requires mud-
dling around in the emotional debris of change. It is not that this
type wants to avoid, mislead, or falsely act, it is that he values
urgency over consideration. What he didn't know (or didn't feel the
need to know) *can* hurt him." This kind of BSer has been conditioned into expressing and acting out a ritualized false optimism.
Developmental efforts work much better with an uninformed optimist than a true hard-core BSer. The hard core have much deeper
and more fundamental learning blockages. Ideas for intervention:

- Find ways to place BSers in long-term, intense interaction
with learners—that is, those who have successfully adopted new and
more relevant ways of being in the organization. This can be done
through task forces, job assignments, or mentoring relationships.

- Force inside-out development. The key to removing the
blockage lies inside the BSer. This makes the primary development
intrapersonal—an examination of internal drives, identity, needs,
and interpersonal agenda. These are deep and difficult learnings,
but offer the only real payoffs. Laboratory training including T-
groups, simulations, deep coaching, and counseling are all legiti-
mate interventions, as is encouraging outside therapy.

- Connect BSers with outside organizations—customers, sup-
pliers, or exemplars of best practice—that are doing a good job of
organizational learning. This connection should again be grounded
in concrete, measurable and quantitative goals.

A Tale of Two Regions

The leasing division of a national financial services organization
decided to reorganize and move from six to eight regions. The division president broke set and actually used their succession planning
system. He and the vice president of human resources interviewed a
number of their *hi-pos*, employees designated as having high potential, and selected the top two. Their top candidate, Hugh, although
having less than a year's tenure with the organization, was a natural.

He had industry experience from his past job with a competitor, was assertive, and came across, in the words of the president, as "sales and customer oriented." He fit right into the outgoing marketing culture of the division.

The second choice was not so easy. In fact, had it not been for the advocacy of the human resource vice president, Mary might not have received the offer. She was reserved, analytical, and female in an organization that was extroverted, seat-of-the-pants, and macho. She accomplished two firsts with her promotion: she was the first woman to make regional manager, and the first person ever to make it from the credit side of the business.

Even with the close call on Mary, both seemed excellent choices. They were bright, articulate, and driven to succeed. Hugh had worked in the sales and marketing operations and Mary came from credit. The two top choices thus came from the two major functions of the business.

A regional vice president's job consisted of managing a small staff in a headquarters city and a number of offices spread throughout several states. Hugh went to the Midwest region, which he managed from a Chicago base, and Mary ended up in Atlanta, in the Southeast region. These were action-oriented mainstream assignments, requiring lots of travel and rapid decisions. Regional vice presidents had a lot of autonomy based both on the organizational culture and on the division president's hands-off style.

A few months into Mary's and Hugh's new assignments, the president took a staff job in corporate headquarters. Shortly after his replacement arrived, the strategy changed to larger, more specialized leases. There was less competition in this market niche, but it required customized, nonstandard deals that needed more analysis and a deeper partnership with a smaller number of customers.

Hugh and Mary had not been in their new assignments a year before the layoffs started. First at headquarters—they were startled to find out that the ex-division president was one of the first to go— then throughout the entire extended organization. The leasing division was not immune and quotas and reduction goals came down from headquarters. The truth was that they needed to do something anyway. The new strategy was not improving profits as quickly as had been projected, and they had too many sales and sales support people left over from the old strategy.

The pattern started after a few months, became a trend after a year, and eighteen months into their assignments it was glaringly clear. Hugh was not making it and Mary was becoming a star. Just before their second anniversary as regional vice presidents, Hugh was fired. A few months later, Mary was promoted. Here is what happened in each of the regions:

Midwest Region

From day one Hugh cut a confusing and disruptive swath through the office network. He gave conflicting directions, made customer commitments that could not be met, and so irritated his office managers that some of the more marketable and productive performers left.

When the strategy changed, he immediately ordered the sales people to change their role and develop more custom products. When they had trouble switching gears he quickly reorganized and moved many of the credit analysts to staff and administrative roles in Chicago. This had a twofold effect: it increased his overhead expense, and it left the offices with no skilled staff.

The Midwest region came in first in only one thing during Hugh's tenure: layoffs. He exceeded his goals; he cut more people in less time than anyone in the division. True to form, he had a bad process with no participation and horrible communications. He topped it off by paying no attention to the survivors.

Southeast Region

Mary took it slow at first. She visited all the offices, listened to her people, and developed a core of competent and very loyal subordinates.

She reacted to the strategic change by investing in training and helping the sales people change their skills. She moved most of the credit experts out of the Atlanta headquarters and into the field offices.

She found ways through attrition and planned retirements to reduce her layoff quota. Her numbers were so good that she was actually able to renegotiate her reduction goals. Those few people that did have to leave were treated with dignity and respect. She and her staff worked hard on communications and on helping the survivors.

What happened? How could these two hi-pos take such divergent courses of action? The answer is that Hugh was a BSer, and Mary was a learner. This story illustrates three things:

• Without careful initial analysis, learners and BSers look very much the same! Enthusiasm, energy, and decisiveness are traits shared by both groups. It is an irony of behavioral science measurement systems that there are times when the worst group shares many of the same traits as the best group.

• It is important to look beneath the surface to smoke out the BSers. Had the president talked to Hugh's subordinates or had the human resources vice president done a more thorough reference check with his previous employer, Hugh probably would not have been hired—and certainly would not have ended up on the top of the hi-po list.

• BSers always act according to R-BS behavior patterns and learners always behave in congruence with R-learning behavior. Without some form of intervention, people do behave according to type. In the case of Mary and Hugh, the behavior played out quickly and clearly. There are situations with more buffers and intervening variables when R-type behavior takes longer to emerge. But it will emerge! Learners will find ways to help the organization, and BSers will, left to their own devices, find ways to hinder it.

Encountering the BSer: Up Close and Personal

Again, in the section that follows, the reader will find tips for dealing with bosses and employees who exhibit the BS response pattern. Also included are tips for those who perceive their own behavior as reflective of the BS pattern.

If You Work for One

If your boss operates with a BS response type you have that most basic choice of higher life forms: fight or flight! If you choose to fight, your chances of remaining sane and productive are greatly enhanced if you are able to do one or both of the following:

• Find work that distances you from your boss. This distance can be physical (you can travel a lot or work in a remote site); technical (you can have a job where the BSer boss doesn't understand your task, your tools, or your technology); or psychological (you can choose not to get hooked and repress, deny, and deflect his influence). Establishing the psychological distance is difficult for most people, and it will only work in the short term.

• Find a protector; a person at or above your boss's level who will run interference for you and cut you some slack.

If it appears that you are stuck in a long-term relationship with a BSer boss and you can't either escape into work or find a protector, you are strongly advised to get out and get out soon. BSers are not just toxic to organizational systems, they are hazardous to the health of those who report to them.

If One Works for You

Here are some ideas if you uncover a BSer in your reporting chain:

• Do some introspection. Have you known it for a while and not acted, seduced by that decisiveness and positive attitude? Did it make you feel good to have someone in your organization who seemed to know what to do and took action without complaining?

If these questions hit home, look around at the rest of your staff—there may be more! Don't let your need for a positive, affirming, and action-oriented employee allow you to turn a BSer loose in your organization. It is definitely not worth the risk.

• Decide if there is enough developmental payoff to compensate for the pain. You have to make a develop-or-outplace decision.

• Move quickly to rein in the BSer's power: remove line management or people management duties and limit autonomy. Work to structure the necessary high-impact developmental assignments described earlier in this chapter.

If You Are One

If you find yourself residing in the lower right corner of the R-factor model, take heart. Your awareness that you live in that place is a strong indicator that you're on your way out! Most BSers are not blessed with self-awareness, so your discovery is a very good sign. In fact, so few hard-core BSers are able to self-diagnose that there is a fair probability that you may not be one at all. You may be an uninformed optimist, and in this case, your R-BS behavior is a result of cultural conditioning and lack of awareness. Uninformed optimists are always easier to help than hard-core BSers.

Regardless of whether you are of the hard-core or the uninformed optimist variety, you need to get some help. Awareness is a first step, but is never sufficient. The most powerful form of help is the most painful for it involves confronting your internal drives, fears, and anxieties. It is difficult, but it is absolutely worth the agony. You only have one life and you are in all probability further into it than you realize. Now is the time to get on with it.

The BSer: Perspective and Observations

Although only making up a relatively small proportion of the workforce, the BS response type represents a particularly difficult challenge for leaders attempting to revitalize organizations. There are issues in two areas—identification and development.

BSers are difficult to spot, at least initially. It is easy for a busy and committed organizational leader to be seduced and flattered by the BSers' can-do, action orientation. Since at first blush they appear very similar to the type of employee managers definitely want to empower—the learner—it is easy to make a mistake. Because it is clearly not in the organization's best interest to put BSers in high-impact roles, leaders need to learn to look deeper than surface behavior and attitude. The best way to ferret out BSers is to talk to their past peers and those who have worked for them. It may feel awkward or even mistrusting to take the time for an internal reference check if the person is inside the organization, or to press for more information on an outside hire, but it is indeed worth the effort.

BSers present a very difficult challenge for leaders who like to help people grow and who are developmentally optimistic. BSers are not good for the organization and are difficult to change. Even the most hard-wired, developmentally optimistic leader needs to consider the expedient solution of getting the BSer out of the organization. Difficult though it may be for some leaders, firing hard-core BSers is, unfortunately, often the best solution for the organization.

As noted, there are two types of BSers: the uninformed optimist and the true hard core. The uninformed optimist has been conditioned into the BS response pattern and can be conditioned out of it. Such a person is in many ways similar to those who have become the victims of cults. Early work experience, strong BS-type bosses, and one-dimensional, charismatic organizational cultures combine with a compliant personality, the need for absolutes, and an unhealthy desire for approval from others to condition some employees into ritualized behavior patterns. The end result is a person who reacts to change with thoughtless optimism and moves into action without plan or theory. The good news is that many of these uninformed optimists can be deprogrammed and taught to learn and think for themselves.

The hard-core BSers are a different kettle of fish, or more appropriately, a different crock of you-know-what. Their ability to learn and adapt is fundamentally blocked. This blockage seems to be connected to their self-esteem, early childhood experience, and fear of vulnerability. Helping them is a much more difficult and protracted operation.

Organizational leaders are not psychiatrists and they have to accept employees the way they find them, complete with self-esteem deficits, early childhood scars, and vulnerability to charismatic conditioning. The task of the leader dealing with an employee exhibiting the R-BS behavior pattern is to help that person learn how to learn. This is not an easy task since the only real solution involves a combination of deep insight, behavior modeling, and gradual movement reinforced by coaching, feedback, and support. This is why authentically helping the hard-core BSer is so difficult for even the best manager.

5

The Learner

Learners defiantly live on the right side of the tracks. They can be found in the upper right corner of the R-factor model, a place where we would all like to reside. It is an exclusive neighborhood with only two requisites for citizenship: a high capacity for change and a high level of comfort with that change.

Learners actively respond to transitions. As shown in Figure 5.1, they engage the issues and grow as people.

Learners are the primary wielders of the new glue. They, however, are more than simple mixers, bearers, and users. In an existential sense, they *are* the adhesive—they hold organizations together. Learners are what separate organizations that will grow and thrive from those that will wither and die. Without a critical mass of people who have the ability to learn from experience, organizations will indeed fall apart.

Past competitive differentiators—access to capital, technology, and control over critical natural resources—are all increasingly irrelevant. In the global, borderless, and often copyrightless networked kaleidoscope that constitutes the new reality, the only thing that will separate the winners from the losers will be the quality of the human—not the inhuman—resources. The people who will make the difference will not be the overwhelmed, the entrenched, or the BSers; they will be learners.

Figure 5.1. The Learner: High Capacity for Change, High Comfort with Change.

The Learner

Engaging
and
Growing

Of *Homo Sapiens* and Organization Charts

Although there is a symbiotic relationship between learners—that is, humans with flesh, blood, passion, and messy unpredictability, and learning organizations—systems with no inherent spirit or soul—we too often mix the concepts. Unless we are very careful, we fall into the trap of assigning human properties to organizations: *reifying* them. We likewise conceptualize people as Spock-like automatons who can be managed as though they have no human spirit or individuality. At the existential level, people are all there is; there ain't no more! At this level, organizations are nothing more than shared abstractions that do not exist beyond the sum of individual behaviors within some form of preagreed, arbitrary boundaries.

Organizations do have a very powerful role in stimulating human learning, development, and creativity. This is an enabling and reinforcing process that occurs in a collective environment. Any time groups of humans gather together, shared—often implicit—agreements evolve around norms, values, and behavior. It is in the mixing of this subtle, ambiguous, often nonverbal soup of individual values and perspectives with others—in the collective—that organizational cultures are born. Drath and Palus (1993) argue that the process of creating meaning in a collective environment is the essence of the leadership process.

Rodney's Reactionary Reification

Whenever I find myself falling in the trap of assigning human properties to organizational systems I think of Rodney's attempt to play intellectual systems games when his organization was falling apart. He was known throughout his organization as the quality guru. He wasn't an official guru in the sense of a Deming, a Crosby, or a Juran; he was simply an electrical engineer who had kept his surfboard afloat on the treacherous wave of Total Quality Management. In the Midwest computer software and components manufacturing company where he worked, the quality wave was treacherous because it was so political, and when others who were surfing on that same wave wiped out on the bureaucratic shoals, Rodney emerged as the top staff officer in charge of quality. This was a very powerful and influential position in the organization. Unfortunately, Rodney was a permanent resident of the lower right box. He was a career BSer.

Rodney reported to the CEO, who (to give him the benefit of the doubt) believed in quality in the abstract but chose not to dirty his hands with details or understanding. He therefore made a few speeches, sent out a few internal memos, and handed out a lot of wall plaques and other trinkets—what Rodney called "quality awards." Mainly, the CEO delegated the corporation's quality efforts to Rodney.

Rodney's company was in the process of living out the old adage "what goes up, must come down"—and they were coming down a lot faster than they had ascended. They had ridden the innovation and proprietary technology of a few creative founders and enjoyed a steep and invigorating growth curve for six years. When the technology grew stale and the founders cashed out, the organization stopped growing, floundered for a year, and began an accelerating nose dive. Customer expectations had changed as a result of new technology, vicious global competition had emerged, and the organization was stuck with a fixed cost structure they couldn't support. They badly needed a new strategy, new products, and a new culture. They had had the predictable rounds of layoffs, and R-entrenched employees formed the majority of their surviving workforce. The number of overwhelmed employees was also growing steadily, as the entrenched lost hope and dropped out. What few learners remained were stretched and approaching burnout. The organization was spinning out of control and the only ones steering were Rodney and his fellow BSers—who kept it spinning by propelling it with gusto in uncoordinated and contradictory directions.

Rodney was given too much power by the CEO, who, it was eventually discovered, had found his personal escape in alcohol. Rodney channeled this power into slogans, trinkets, programs, systems measuring activity and not results, and a complex and unending web of reports, meetings, and institutionalized pep talks that were as shallow in meaning as they were boisterous in delivery. Rodney's solution to the organization's problems was to establish a crazy quilt of unconnected programs and slogan-driven activities that piled stress onto the remaining learners and caused the entrenched to hunker even further down in the trenches.

My first and last formal meeting with Rodney was set up by one of the few learners who worked in Rodney's chain of command. True to the optimistic character of his R-type, he had organized the session in an attempt to put some focus in Rodney's form-over-substance approach to cultural change. I attended not from any optimistic belief that I could help Rodney—I've had too much experience with his R-type—but because of my friendship with his staff member and the fact that he claimed that Rodney had read one of my books and I could be supportive. The third person to join us in this meeting with Rodney was a consultant who specialized in organizational learning.

It was a bizarre meeting. As we entered Rodney's office, I noticed his desk. Atop towering piles of correspondence, bound reports, unread *Wall Street Journals*, and empty Styrofoam coffee cups sat three books: Hammer and Champy's *Reengineering the Corporation* (1993); Senge's *The Fifth Discipline* (1990); and, nestled humbly among these two giants, my own *Healing the Wounds* (1993). It turned out Rodney really hadn't read these books but had skimmed summaries prepared by his staff. With his engineer's orientation, he was attempting to relate Hammer and Champy's process redesign, Senge's systems thinking, and level four of my pyramid intervention model. He not only wanted to connect them on a matrix, but, as a next step, to turn the product into a program that could be translated into quantifiable goals and factored into the organization's performance management system!

Relating process reengineering, level four interventions, and systems thinking is a stimulating and interesting idea; in some ways they are about the same thing. Such an effort, however, would at least initially be best accomplished by a graduate student or a management theorist. Certainly, given the prognosis of Rodney's organization, such an effort was not the wisest use of management time!

Rodney communicated in monologues. When he was five minutes into his introductory speech, an analogy just popped into my head. I blurted out:

"Rodney, trying to hook those three concepts together and integrate them into an organizationwide measurement system at this point in your organization's history is like a surgeon doing an analysis of three different medical textbooks when his patient is dying on the operating table! You need to save the patient, then worry about theory and measurement matrices."

"But the organization needs an integrated system," I remember Rodney responding. In fact, almost all of Rodney's comments were prefaced by "The organization needs" or "The organization is looking for" preambles. When he gave us "The organization feels," I had to interrupt again.

"The organization can't feel, Rodney. Only people can do that. Organizations are things, not people, in fact they don't really exist at all in a philosophical sense. They are only shared abstractions inside our heads," I continued, knowing I had violated one of my own consulting rules by working my agenda and not the client's—and feeling good about it anyway.

I don't remember much more about that meeting except that it lasted a long time, which was not a surprise, and had a relatively positive outcome, which was a surprise. The learning organizational consultant got the go-ahead to do a workshop with a particularly needy and important part of the organization. Rodney eventually left the organization and started, of all things, his own quality improvement consulting firm. I have been told he has developed an impressive list of clients who, no doubt, are paying him a lot of money for his impressive array of disconnected activity. His former organization is now much smaller and although marginally profitable is still burdened with an entrenched workforce and a heavy cost structure.

Five Learnings from Rodney

- Confronting a BSer without a clear power base does not work and will not serve the learners in the organization well. The meeting had a positive result despite my contribution, not because of it.

- Organizations populated by entrenched and overwhelmed employees are vulnerable to programs and systems that are long on slogans, activity for activity's sake, trinkets, and meaningless measurement systems. The future bodes well for Rodney's consulting business.

- Assigning human properties to organizational systems is a cop-out that we all have to guard against. It is a safe escape into the impersonal and avoids the necessary pain of dealing with people—with all their warm, messy humanness.

- Helping lead organizations out of the woods is a task of the heart as well as the head. Rodney's attempt to connect and measure three models, though intellectually stimulating, was not what the organization needed.

- Learners are vulnerable and an empowered BSer can indeed put them in the outs; as in *drive* out or *burn*out!

Discovering Learners

It is relatively easy to spot overwhelmed, entrenched, and BSing employees. For one thing, they constitute the majority of the workforce; for another, we find it easier and somewhat cathartic to focus on negative traits and behaviors. We often have a harder time with learners. Their behavior and underlying traits are less flamboyant than those of BSers, less pathological than the overwhelmed, and less aggressive than the entrenched. They are frequently immersed in their work and out of sight. The ability to learn from experience and the skill to let go of the old and venture into an ambiguous future armed with nothing more than self-esteem and a positive attitude are powerful traits, but not easy to spot at the water cooler or the coffee machine. A few overwhelmed organizations have come to doubt whether they had any learners at all. Although in some cultures they are hard to discover, I have yet to find an organization with no learners and estimate that most have a range of from 5 to 20 percent.

The R-Factor Contrast Exercise

We use an exercise that clients have found very helpful not only for discovering learners in their organizations, but also as a powerful reinforcement of the validity of the R-factor model itself. It is a very simple exercise and is included here because it can be done without extensive facilitation and with predictable results that can energize employees. It works best in small groups—up to ten participants per group. I have used it in one small group of four executives and with audiences well into the hundreds.

The first step involves dividing the group in half. If there are ten people, make two small groups of five. If there are two hundred people, divide the room into two sets of subgroups of ten each. The first part of the exercise is done individually. Each person is instructed to take out a pen or pencil and something to write on. Half the room gets the following instructions:

> Think of a person in your organization. It can be someone you work closely with or someone you just know. This person is doing an exceptional job and is really helping with the transition. This is the kind of person about whom you can say 'I wish we had more like her or him! If we had a whole department full of people like that we could do anything! If we had an entire organization made of people like that we would be world beaters. This is the kind of person we need to make the transition really work!' Think of an actual person, get a fix on him or her. Now, without using names, write down what this person is like: how they act; what they do; how they behave. List some of their important traits.

The other half of the group gets these instructions:

> Think of an actual person in your organization. It can be someone you work closely with or someone you just

know. This person may have done a good job in the past, but not now! This person is having a very hard time with the transition. This is the kind of a person about whom you can say 'We don't need any more like her or him! If we had a whole department full of people like that we'd really be stuck. If we had an entire organization filled with people like that we'd be in big trouble. We can't make the transition work with people like that!' Think of an actual person, get a fix on him or her. Now, without using names, write down what this person is like: how they act; what they do; how they behave. List some of their important traits.

After a few minutes of individual work, each small group is asked to share their lists and come up with a group profile. They are next invited to share their profile with the entire group. This sharing rotates between groups who describe those making a good transition, and those who are describing the opposite.

What materializes from half of the room are descriptions of the overwhelmed, the entrenched, and the BS response patterns. In most cases these descriptions are so spot-on it is frightening (this exercise is generally done before any discussion of the R-factor).

The product of the other half are descriptions of learners. These, too, are instructive.

- Despite type of industry, whether the organization is profit or nonprofit, military or civilian, religious or secular, and regardless of size or location, the same three traits are described:

  Learners are seen as optimistic and positive.

  They possess a can-do attitude and are willing to engage the issues and take action.

  They exhibit a sense of perspective and humor.

- There are learners in all organizations. Even the most overwhelmed organizations seem able to discover and identify their key learners in the small amount of time spent reflecting in this exercise.

- Learners are an endangered species. Organizational managers in overwhelmed and entrenched organizations perceive that their learners are extremely vulnerable to burnout. Since they are marketable and are not afraid of taking risks, learners are valued in the external market and many choose to leave toxic organizational cultures.

I have facilitated this exercise in a large number of settings in many different countries, types of organization, levels, and geographic regions. The consistency of descriptions of all four R-types is remarkable.

Learners: Four Dimensions

As was the case with the other three R-types, I will present four perspectives of the learning response pattern: their feelings, their typical reactions to transitions, their learning behavior, and their needs in regard to successfully surviving transitions. I will again include some typical descriptions distilled from clients and program participants.

How Learners Feel

Challenged, stretched, and optimistic. As shown in Figure 5.1, the learners' basic response pattern is to engage and grow. During transitions, learners engage the issues and work hard to help find positive outcomes. Joining the fray—engaging—is hard, challenging work, and acquiring and applying the necessary new learning—growing—requires a stretch even for the best learner. Learners approach this difficult, challenging work in a positive, optimistic manner. Unlike the overwhelmed and the entrenched, learners don't often complain! Typical descriptions:

> "I really like working for him. He works long hours on tough projects, but he is always up and when he's up it helps the rest of us."

> "Now that we have to work closer to the customer I'm very happy that she went out there and found out what they truly need. I had to cover for her when she was gone, but now it's making all our jobs easier. I'd like some more employees like her!"

> "He's positive and he always tries. You can't say that about a lot of people around here."

Comfortable with the need for change. Learners accept the need to let go of the old and move into a changed and ambiguous future. Unlike the BSer, who is equally comfortable with change, the learner understands the challenge and still moves forward. This is a courageous act. The learner has faced the twin demons of uncertainty and ambiguity and still takes action—while the BSer blunders into the new reality blindly, repressing and not confronting the demons. Typical descriptions:

> "I like the way she keeps us pressing on . . . she knows we have to do things differently and lets us know too."

> "He's a cool customer. Knows what we've got to do, accepts it, and gets on with it."

> "Three years ago, I never would have thought she would be so strong. She's found a way to adjust and keep moving . . . I like the way she does it without all that complaining."

Have the power of positive doing. Learners engage, and they engage in a positive manner. They want to make a difference and they are not afraid to get their hands dirty in the process. Typical descriptions:

> "She makes things happen and I can tell it makes her feel good."

> "He's like an old fashioned cattle drover . . . heads us up and moves us out, even rounds up a few strays."

> "That transition team has taken a damn mess and made something out of it and I don't know how they did it, but hats off to them."

In control of their own destiny. Learners are internally directed. Their confidence and ability to shrug off setbacks and naysayers is a behavioral manifestation of their self-esteem and internal locus of control. This self-efficacy is a primary distinguishing trait of learners. Typical comments:

> "She's like that battery commercial, just keeps on going, and going, and going."

> "Stubborn is not the right word. I'd say committed and very strong. He is not going to let them grind him down!"

> "He's above all that whining and bitching . . . it's like water off a duck's back."

Not afraid of short-term mistakes or setbacks. Because of their self-confidence, learners are able to take risks without fear of personal consequences. A core competence in true learners is their ability to accept short-term setbacks or deterioration in performance in anticipation of long-term gains. Typical descriptions:

"While everyone else is keeping their head down, she's stand-ing up there directing traffic. She doesn't worry about getting shot."

"It took them a while and things were snarled up for longer than we liked . . . but now they've got it right and I think we are going to be a much better staff function for it."

"He was fat, dumb, and happy, not to mention safe out here in the line. I don't know why he took that corporate job in today's climate . . . but he did and he is doing some good there."

How Learners React to Transitions

Find the silver linings behind the dark clouds. Learners find positive out-comes in what others see as negative situations. This ability to mine the positive nuggets from turmoil and change is a hallmark of the learning response. Typical descriptions:

"She helped us see the 'up' of downsizing."

"The reason . . . they do so well is that they are positive and like the freedom and challenge . . . that goes along with everything being up for grabs."

"He learned to like it when they wiped out the corporate staff. He found all the action in the division more fun."

Find humor in difficult situations and use it as a tool. Learners have the ability to laugh at the situation and use humor as a way to relieve stress and provide perspective. This is not the cynical or destructive humor often found with the entrenched or the over-whelmed. Learners consciously use humor as a positive force to reduce tension and anxiety. Even in the most trying times, many learners are relaxed and cheerful. Typical descriptions:

"She has always got a smile on her face and that helps the rest of us relax a bit."

"It's nice to hear laughter again . . . I just like coming to these meetings for that reason alone."

"He knows just the right time to be playful—to lighten things up."

Are very aware of both strengths and weaknesses. Learners are self-aware, and in times of change and stress they use their strengths while at the same time working to shore up their weaknesses. Typical descriptions:

"Unlike a lot of them, he didn't try to fake it. He went out and learned it on his own. Now he knows more about using PCs than almost anyone here."

"She has super interpersonal skills and that really helps, but she can't charm her way through that job . . . give her credit she can do the tough stuff too. She didn't have to do that before and she has proven she can do it."

"He's exceptionally good at selling. He knows it . . . he knows we need it this year, and he is working his ass off to get it done for us."

Expand the boundaries of their personal comfort zone. The learner's primary response patterns are engaging and growing. Growing involves expanding boundaries and pushing beyond safe limitations. Typical descriptions:

"When we decentralized, it made us drop corporate review and approval of new credit lines. It was hard for all of us who were used to that, but some of us learned to live without it, we found better things to do with our time."

"None of us liked working with new people and a different system, but the best people on either side found a way to accommodate the merger."

"I never thought she could handle a department that big and a couple years ago she probably would have failed, but she found a way."

How Learners Operate

Pay attention to the learning process, the how of learning. True learners are aware of how they learn. This is a differentiating trait from non-learners. Typical descriptions:

"She didn't just read the manual, she asked, bounced her ideas off us old-timers. She said she learned a lot that way."

"I used to jump in with both feet and pick it up as I went along. That only works for some things and I know that I've got to do some thinking and talking first if I'm going to be effective in this new job."

Grow through developmental surrender. Unlike the entrenched, learners don't fight change. They know that, difficult though it may be, letting go of the unproductive old and wallowing in unfamiliar ambiguity will result in new learnings. This surrendering of the old ways to an uncertain future outcome requires confidence and self-esteem; two central traits of the learner. Typical comments:

"I didn't know where we were going or how we were going to get there, but I sure knew that what we were doing wasn't going to do it. So, I just took a risk. No one knew I was making it up as we went along."

"Well, let's say I had faith that there was light at the end of the tunnel and even though it got pretty black, we sure as hell couldn't turn back."

"Some of those meetings . . . it was like the blind leading the blind. But, you know, we had faith that we could find an answer."

Strive to solve problems rather than place blame. Learners engage at the problem-solving level and don't personalize issues. In this regard, they behave according to a basic precept of most Total Quality Management models, and blame the system and not the individual. Typical descriptions:

"She dug right in. Didn't waste a lot of useless time, like the last boss, going on witch hunts, trying to figure out who screwed up."

"It feels good spending our energy trying to beat the competition and not beating on each other, and we don't do much of that now that he took over the division."

"I 'fessed up, but he didn't want to hear about it being my fault. Wanted to work on making it right. That got me. I'd walk off a cliff for him now!"

Willing to fill gaps in personal development. Learners are willing, at times driven, to work at personal development. They often do this at the expense of their non-work life. Typical descriptions:

"I thought it would be a hard sell to get her into language training but she was anxious to do it and willing to pay the price at home of doing it at night. She is doing a much better job over there now because of it."

"He didn't have to take that assignment and we both knew moving to a staff role would be hard for him. He did it, paid his dues, and when it's over he will come back to the line much better for it—and he'll have made an impact, too."

"All you need to do is tell her what she needs and then the best thing to do is get out of the way. She's hard-wired to get it done."

What Learners Need to Be Successful Survivors

Protection from attempting to be all things to all people. Learners are vulnerable to burnout: they are scarce, important resources and everyone wants a piece of them. They are often involved in important transitional projects while simultaneously attempting to save the overwhelmed, encourage the entrenched, and rein in the power of the BSers. Learners are driven to make a difference. Unless they are careful, they can engage and grow themselves into ineffectiveness. Learners are susceptible to a special form of combat fatigue that puts them into a category called the *overwhelmed learner*. Overwhelmed learners do not move diagonally across the model into the lower left box, since they have the requisite ability to learn and comfort with change; they simply grow weary and temporarily stop trying or, often, leave the organization. Ideas for intervention:

• Boundary setting and symptom awareness. Learners respond well to data. Often making learners aware of their impossible workload, helping them set limits, and giving them feedback as to signs of burnout is all that is necessary.

• Healthful activities. Exercise, proper sleep, vacations, and managing excessive work hours are all antidotes to the condition of overwhelmed learner.

• R and R assignments and projects. Even combat troops are given leave and sent back for rest and relaxation from time to time. Learners, too, are in a form of combat and need to be given a break. Conferences, seminars, special nonstressful staff assignments, and trips to locations out of town or out of the country are examples of ways to temporarily get the learner off the front line.

Latitude, air time, and assignments with impact. The lights of learners should not be hidden under organizational blankets; they should be allowed to shine. Learners are the primary assets organizations employ to facilitate successful transitions. They need to be given space, visibility, and key assignments that are important to the organization. Learners are just the opposite of BSers: they need to be empowered!

• Skip-level assignments. If learners are two or three levels below the real action, now is the time to promote them. A high-potential learner is not optimized sitting on the bench or languishing on a back-up chart in someone's file drawer. Organizations need to take risks with learners. Why stay with an entrenched or an overwhelmed performer in a key assignment when you have learners on the bench? It makes no sense. Bench the entrenched and put the learner on the front line. They will both do better!

• Quality air time. Learners often have a good grasp of the problem and lots of ideas about what to do about it. They need to be given forums to communicate their ideas and need to be listened to. Special study assignments with presentations to decision-making groups in top management, responsibility for developing and communicating important plans and strategies, and one-on-one discussions with key leaders are examples.

• Ward off the bureaucracy. Empowered learners working hard to turn the organization around don't need to be nibbled to death by entrenched rules administrators. Those in influence can provide needed relief by letting the learners do their thing and running interference against the bureaucracy.

Rewards and reinforcement. Learners have an internal locus of control and are motivated by the work itself and not by hygiene factors such as pay or recognition (Hertzberg, 1964). On the other hand, they are human, are susceptible to burnout, have families asking them why they work so hard, and do need to have their hygiene needs addressed.

• Give them a lot of recognition and public strokes. This visibility helps them and, more important, it helps others. The other employees know who the learners are, and public recognition helps reinforce the idea that the good guys get recognized. This is motivational for those hesitant to take the risks necessary to begin a journey toward the upper right box.

• Pay them well. Again, money doesn't motivate, but the lack of feeling fairly paid can demotivate. Learners should feel fairly rewarded and should not have to leave the organization to experience this feeling.

Developmental roles and assignments. Learners are both driven to engage and help the organization, and to grow and develop personally. To keep learners motivated and prevent their jumping ship, organizations need to satisfy their personal growth needs.

• Consciously find assignments that are developmental. The Center for Creative Leadership's research on learning assignments, *Lessons of Experience* (McCall, Lombardo, and Morrison, 1988), outlines a number of developmental assignments: changes in scope or scale, shifts from line to staff, start-ups, fix-its, expatriate roles, and turnarounds. When learners are given key front-line developmental assignments, there is a double payoff—the learners gain relevant skills and become even more of a competitive edge, and the organization gets a learner in an important position.

• Place young and developing learners under the tutelage of older, more experienced learners. Young learners need to work for old learners; it is a mutually complementary relationship. The young learners get their need for development and coaching met and the experienced learners have the opportunity to be mentors. It is never a good idea to put young learners under control-oriented BSers or entrenched employees.

Learners: Five Frequent Questions

What follows are five of the most frequent and interesting questions I hear concerning those exhibiting R-learning behavior:

QUESTION: It sounds like learners are superwomen and men. Can they really do all that?

ANSWER: Actually, learners are quite vulnerable, very human, and they have the normal quotient of warts and blemishes. What differentiates them, however, are the three behaviors described in the R-factor contrast exercise earlier in this chapter: they are optimistic and positive, have a can-do attitude coupled with engaging the issues by taking action, and they have a sense of humor and perspective. At first glance, these descriptions seem fairly trite and banal. They certainly, thank god, are not the type of obscure jargon found in some academic journals. If you look a bit deeper, you will discover that they are very powerful descriptors of behaviors that are in short supply in many organizations, particularly those going through the trauma of fundamental change. If I were starting a business with my money, I'd want a critical mass of people with those behaviors and I wouldn't worry about competition.

QUESTION: Are you really talking about ability to learn and comfort with change, or are you just describing a person with a positive, buoyant personality who may or may not be able to deal with the complexities of the new reality?

ANSWER: We're not talking a Forrest Gump here! Learners have a positive outlook, but they also have the ability to learn and adapt. There is a type of BSer described in Chapter Four as an uninformed optimist who fits the profile outlined in the question, but that is certainly not a true learner. Learners know how to learn and have the courage to let go of the old without a clear compass to guide them into the future.

QUESTION: Most of the examples you use are managers and executives. Are there learners at other levels of the organization?

ANSWER: Most of the people I work with are managers and executives, so those examples come naturally. I also have the perspective that learners can exert the most leverage in key front-line management roles. This is not to say that there aren't learners at all levels in organizations, there most certainly are. In fact, I have seen many examples of nonexempt learners in times of trauma providing leadership that goes far beyond their job descriptions or labor department classifications.

QUESTION: Are learners smarter than the other types?

ANSWER: It seems to me to have more to do with EQ, emotional quotient (Goleman, 1995) than IQ. There also seems to be a connection with self-esteem and self-efficacy.

QUESTION: Can you develop learners and, if so, how do you do that?

ANSWER: Yes, you can. The "hows" of developing learners are discussed in Chapter Nine.

Encountering the Learner: Up Close and Personal

This section provides tips for interacting with bosses and employees who are learners. It also offers ideas for those readers who themselves are learners.

If You Work for One

If your boss is a learner, you are fortunate regardless of your type. If you are overwhelmed, the boss will try to stop you from sinking and attempt to help you gain some control and symptom relief. If you are entrenched, you will get help in taking the necessary small steps toward the coveted residences in the upper right box of the model. If you are a BSer, you will not like the managerial actions, but they are in service of the organization's best interests—and your own. A learner boss will rein in your power and hold you accountable for some limited, quantifiable objectives. You will also get a good, close look into a mirror even though you may not accept what you see. If you are a fellow learner, you and your boss can bond and connect over doing the kind of good, challenging, and helpful work that will make things better for the organization. You can also give your boss feedback in regard to overwork and potential burnout. The good thing about learners working together is that they can help each other avoid ending up as overwhelmed learners.

If One Works for You

If you, too, are a learner you'll have the simpatico relationship described in the previous paragraph. If you're a different type, life may not be so easy either for you or your employee. If you are overwhelmed, particularly if you are an outward-bound overwhelmed, it won't make much difference. Chances are, you have no influence or control over your people anyway. The good news is that your employee may try to coach you! If this happens, listen—you may get some real help. If you're entrenched, you may get into a power game. This is almost guaranteed to happen if you have strong control needs and are unwilling to let your learner-employee try the new behavior you are avoiding. The best advice to you is to let go. Control contests won't work in the long run, learners either transfer out or quit. If you cut some slack, you just might do yourself and the organization some good in the process. If you are a BSer and you supervise a learner, you are making life miserable! The learner will either wait for you to crash or find a way to get out from under your control. If you suspect you may be a BSer and have a learner working for you, watch how your employee copes and engages. You may be able to take some small steps yourself.

If You Are One

You are, obviously, doing a lot of things right. Your main task is to be vigilant for signs of burnout. You don't want to be an overwhelmed learner. That won't do you or the organization any good. Find ways to get continuing valid feedback on your stress and life-balance. Even the best learner has blind spots when she is focused on doing what comes naturally: engaging and growing.

The Learner: Perspective and Observations

Every organization wants a workforce made up of people who have a high comfort with change and the ability to learn and grow. This gives them the ultimate competitive advantage and ensures their future. Unfortunately, many of those organizations who need learners the most have organizational climates that drive them out. It is an interesting dance, a chicken-and-egg issue. Do organizations with cultures conducive to learning develop people with the capacity to learn how to learn, or do learners develop learning organizations? It is a fascinating—and in the final analysis distracting—debate. What is, is; organizations are where they are. The task of organizational leaders is to make things better and that involves the crucial task of ensuring that there is a critical mass of people with the drive to engage the issues with action and the ability to develop their own learning competence.

Developing, selecting, and preserving learners is a complex task that does not lend itself to simple prescriptive answers. The currency of the realm involves such complex variables as self-esteem, risk taking, ability to go against the grain of one's own comfort level, and emotional maturity.

Part III

Relating Individual and Organizational R-Types

6

Assessing Organizational R-Types

The classic put-down definition of a consultant as someone from out of town with a briefcase had some truth to it, but—as is the case with other stereotypes from the old paradigm—it is changing. With the proliferation of consultants in the new reality, many don't need to leave their hometown to ply their trade, and the briefcase is frequently replaced by the laptop. One thing remains constant: consultants are professional outsiders who spend a great deal of their working time in other people's organizations. Those of us in these permanent stranger roles often find unique ways to amuse ourselves. As we sit around in conference rooms, cafeterias, or lobbies waiting for the client to show up or the meeting to begin, we play mind games. We may appear sober and professional, but other things are going on in our heads. One of my favorite waiting games is R-type guessing. Is that well-dressed, earnest young executive by the coffee machine really a closet BSer? That disheveled woman bustling through the lobby with a ragged stack of papers and a purposeful look—is she a permanent resident of the entrenched community? And, what about that casually dressed guy making copies and refusing to make eye contact. Is he a shy learner who respects my space, or does he dwell in the lower left box of the overwhelmed?

Another version of the game, the organizational variety, is not played in client offices but in cabs and cars driving through cities, across suburbs, and to and from airports. That modern and shiny new headquarters building off on the left—I wonder if that is the home of a learning organization or if it is the facade of a BS organization? Is that prudish looking building—that aging brick edifice on the corner—the headquarters of an entrenched organization? That ubiquitous glass and steel high-rise off the freeway near the airport—the one with the oversized logo of a Fortune 100 company on the roof line and the for-lease sign on the third floor—is that the regional office of an overwhelmed organization?

Organizational R-Types

Although labeling without data is not a good management or behavioral science practice, R-type guessing in either its individual or organizational form is a relatively harmless amusement as long as it is kept in context. The organizational version of the game, however, is a useful reminder that R-type theory can be extended to organizations.

Because of a lack of hard data and scientific studies, applying the four R-types to organizations is of necessity tentative and subjective. If kept in perspective, however, it can be a very useful diagnostic tool. I have found that organizations, like individuals, appear to show four distinct archetypal response patterns. Figure 6.1 illustrates the four organizational response types.

Overwhelmed Organizations

As is the case with individuals, organizations with both a low readiness to change and a low capacity for change exhibit the overwhelmed response pattern. Their primary coping behavior is withdrawing and avoiding. A good description of the withdrawing and avoiding characteristics of the overwhelmed response pattern is offered by Merry and Brown when they describe the characteristics of declining organizations:

Figure 6.1. Organizational Response Types.

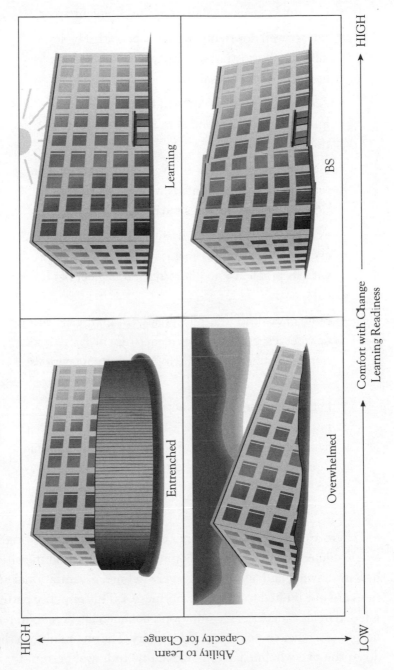

- Negative self-image; failure script of organization.

- Energy well down, organization pervaded by low motivation, frustration, unhappiness, boredom, hopelessness in organization.

- Communication breakdown, interpersonal and intergroup hostility and conflict, distrustful relations, scapegoats.

- Disagreement on goals and values throughout organization, norm disruptment with extreme deviations, organized life loses meaning.

- Pervasive organizational dysfunctioning, production-cycle dysfunctioning; organization unable to cope with its problems; no planning and neglect of physical plant.

- State of decline—outputs greater than inputs; eating up reserves; breakdown of leadership; negative selection of membership; recurring, intensifying periods of crisis.

- High magnitude of dysfunctioning, lack of reserve resources, failure self-image and fear of letting go make change extremely difficult. Rational organizational development methods give no results [1987, pp. 44–45].

There are an enormous number of organizations exhibiting R-overwhelmed behavior, that is, coping with change and transition by withdrawing and avoiding. R-overwhelmed organizational cultures are not limited to for-profit businesses. This response pattern is found in all varieties of organizations: commercial, nonprofit, public, private, religious, fraternal, and military. The end result of a slide down the overwhelmed avoidance and withdrawal pattern for an individual is dropping out of the system. For organizations, it is going out of business, getting acquired, or, for example in a church or college, losing members or students to competing organizations.

Bob's Book Store

The overwhelmed response is not limited to large organizations. Bob and his family operated two book stores in a Midwestern city. When the business started, it was more of a club than a business. It emphasized quality publications, small inventory, and customer intimacy. The early customers would have long and intellectually stimulating discussions with Bob's father and his employees. Even after adding a second store in a suburban location, the firm retained most of its early culture.

Then the market changed: paperbacks, mass merchandising, non–book products, and efficiency became the game. This new reality hit home when a very large national chain opened a megastore in the area. A look at the typical response pattern of the overwhelmed combined with the organizational behavior of Bob's Book Store will illustrate the organizational manifestations of the R-overwhelmed response pattern.

Overwhelmed Responses to Transition

Avoid confronting the real issue. For Bob's Books, the basic issue was the need to change the culture, modernize methods, expand inventory, and diversify the product line. Bob's Books did none of these things. It acted according to type and avoided the real issue. Its primary response was to cut inventories, reduce advertising, and lay off a couple of the newer staff members.

Retreat into old safe patterns. The remaining staff, who were a combination of family members and trusted old-time employees, attempted to work their way out of the problem. They put in longer hours and tried to convince their customers that they would be disloyal if they went elsewhere. This didn't work because the customer demographics had changed and guilt is never a good motivator, even for old and valued customers. Bob's Books staff found that they could not simply work their way out of a fundamental change in the market.

Wait for things to return to normal. The strategy seemed to be to suck it in, tough it out, and wait for the old customers to return. The store could then increase its market share, and things would get back to the way they were. No one, including Bob, really believed this would work—but the norms at Bob's were such that it was perceived as disloyal to speak the truth.

Engage in passive-aggressive behavior. The family members openly pleaded for loyalty and teamwork but privately dissolved into cliques that blamed other family members, the nonfamily employees, and Bob for their troubles.

Avoid thinking about or planning for the future. Since the only strategy was to wait it out and hope things would return to normal, Bob's Books eventually closed—and even that was not done well.

Entrenched Organizations

We are surrounded by organizations of all types that are stuck in outdated old cultures. The struggle to become unstuck is consuming organizations as diverse as IBM and the NAACP. Consider the common theme in these two quotes:

Kwesi Mfume upon his appointment as president and chief executive officer of the NAACP: "We're not going to sit by and watch the world change. We are going to change" (Donnan, 1995).

Luis Gerstner, CEO, IBM: "As far as the culture goes, I haven't been spending time looking back . . . because I don't want it to get me" (Arnst and Verity, 1993).

Both IBM and the NAACP are struggling to let go of exceptionally successful old cultures and survive in very different new realities. Gerstner seems to be making progress in his task of nudging IBM out of the internally oriented fortress of the entrenched. Mfume's task, however, is just beginning. He has the challenge of moving the NAACP back to a position of trust and relevance.

Gerstner is describing a classic entrenched organizational culture when he says, "I have never seen a company that is so introspective, caught up in its own underwear, so preoccupied with internal processes. . . . People in this company tell me it's easier doing business with people outside the company than inside. I would call that an indictment" (Arnst and Verity, 1993).

It's a good-news–bad-news proposition for organizations such as the NAACP and IBM. The good news is that strong leaders such as NAACP's Roy Wilkins and Benjamin Hooks and IBM's Thomas Watson established cohesive cultures that worked and fit the environment of their time. The bad news for Gerstner, Mfume, and many other organizational leaders is that cohesive and historically effective cultures are very difficult to change—no matter how badly they fit the current environment. This struggle to break the grip of a culture that worked in the past but is choking the future is a mark of the new reality and is being waged in almost all organizations. Many of these organizations know what they need to do; they just have a very difficult time doing it. It is the classic entrenched pattern of a high capacity for change combined with a low readiness for change.

Hammer and Champy (1993) capture the paradox of this organizational capacity-readiness mismatch when they write:

> So if managements want companies that are lean, nimble, flexible, responsive, competitive, innovative, efficient, customer focused, and profitable, why are so many American companies bloated, clumsy, rigid, sluggish, noncompetitive, uncreative, inefficient, disdainful of customer needs, and losing money? [p. 7].
>
> Inflexibility, unresponsiveness, the absence of customer focus, an obsession with activity rather than result, bureaucratic paralysis, lack of innovation, high overhead—these are the legacies of one hundred years of American industrial leadership. . . . America's business

problem is that it is entering the twenty-first century with companies designed during the nineteenth century to work well in the twentieth. We need something entirely different [p. 30].

Entrenched organizational cultures operate in all sectors. They are particularly prevalent in newly deregulated organizations (phone companies and public utilities), governments and government agencies, educational systems, health-care systems, the military, many nonprofits, strongly stylized marketing cultures, political parties, and labor unions. What follows is a review of typical entrenched organizational response patterns.

Entrenched Response Patterns

Blame and complain. The survivor-blaming phenomenon (Noer, 1993, p. 68) is alive and well. It has become a permanent part of some organizational cultures. One public utility executive put it this way, "What we are good at here is bitching. It's part of our culture. We bitch about each other, the customers, and the regulators. We do that all day and probably go home at night and bitch to our families too!"

Acknowledge the need to change, but resist changing. The human resources executive of a government agency going through downsizing for the first time drew a picture of a car on a sheet of newsprint. The car was nosed into a brick wall and was in a mud puddle. The driver's mouth was frozen in a grimace and there were droplets of sweat running down his face. The rear wheels of the car were spinning and globs of mud were flying out the rear. When explaining it to his team, he made the point that they all knew they were stuck but were behaving exactly like that driver—keeping the gas pedal to the floor and sinking deeper into the mud. "If we know we're stuck and pushing against a brick wall, why do we keep spinning our wheels? Why don't we try something else?" he challenged his colleagues.

Work harder than ever at previously successful behavior. At a time when quick, responsive decision making and reduced cycle time is the name of the game, many organizations have shown remarkable tenacity at holding on to previously successful processes that will not work in the new reality. Kerry Bunker, a psychologist formerly in the old Bell system, has outlined a ten-step approach to problem solving to illustrate this point. This example is appropriate to a number of other organizations beyond the old Bell system.

Ten-Step Infallible Approach to Problem Solving

- Collect all information that exists on the planet and put in a binder.
- Search for pre-existing binders.
- See who is available and set up a task force.
- Hold a lot of meetings to evaluate the information.
- Develop strategies and plans—conduct numerous pilots.
- Evaluate the results and update the binders (probably need to add a few new binders).
- Cutover to the new process.
- Assume the problem is solved.
- Establish permanent measurement and monitoring systems.
- If all else fails ask for a rate increase [Bunker, 1995].

Try to ride it out until things return to normal. A computer company that grew rapidly by making large mainframe computers missed the opportunity to diversify, develop software, and ride the PC wave. During a planning meeting a senior executive exhorted the group to "hang in there" and "stick to our knitting." This is another version of the traditional battle cry of the entrenched: "We're forgetting what made us great!" In the case of this organization, forgetting what made them great and looking for what would keep them alive would have been a much more useful strategy!

BS Organizations

An organizational culture with a high comfort with change and the inability to learn occupies the lower right quadrant and can be described as a BS organization. These ready-fire-aim organizations are characterized by the BS style of high drive and low substance. Surprisingly, some of these organizations have been able to hang on through some very difficult times, but they will get their due: they are an endangered species. Without some form of protection such as a legislated monopoly or a long-term patent (both are becoming increasingly rare), these organizations will eventually fail. In today's highly competitive, technology-based world, it is impossible to sustain any kind of organization on sizzle and drive alone.

BS organizations seem to fall in five major clusters:

- Organizations with strong, one-dimensional cultures such as low-tech commercial firms with what have been called "rah-rah" sales orientations. Dogmatic religious or fraternal organizations also fall into this cluster.

- Organizations with norms that prevent feedback, dialogue, or questioning the prevalent culture. A totalitarian system such as the former Soviet Union falls into this cluster, as do many businesses still managed by the benevolent despots who started the firms. Leaders in this cluster brook no resistance and tolerate no questioning of their orders.

- Government and political systems where image and smoke-and-mirrors replace service and value-added as the bottom line.

- Temporary, single-issue systems without external feedback systems, and without rewards or reinforcement for diversity or dialogue. Examples include street gangs, some school boards, and juries.

- Entertainment organizations ranging from rock bands to major league baseball.

BS Learning Patterns

The macro organizational system that we call major league baseball (including both the players and the owners) is an outstanding contemporary example of a BS organization. This organization colluded to cause a strike that lasted from August 13, 1994 to April 25, 1995; an action that may have caused irreparable damage to the game by alienating the true customer—the fan. Organized baseball's behavior patterns around this time frame are excellent examples of BS responses.

Block out and ignore the core challenge. BS organizations do not deal with the central issues. They are blind to the core challenges and work on the periphery of the problem. In the case of major league baseball, the core challenge was to find a win-win solution that would restore the fans' faith in the system. This meant the owners had to find a way to contain their own greed and internal bickering. The players faced a similar challenge and needed to understand the limits of collective bargaining by a group of very highly paid entertainers in an artificial system. Both parties behaved according to the R-BS pattern and the result was not a win-win solution. It was a lose-lose-lose solution. The owners lost, the players lost, and they both lost the faith and trust of the customer.

Overestimate strengths, be blind to weaknesses. BS organizational cultures are unable to accurately assess their strengths and are oblivious to their weaknesses. In the baseball strike, the owners thought they could, by a lockout, impose their will on the players. They underestimated the players' tenacity, the fans' irritation, and their own ability to maintain a united front. The players also underestimated the owners' resolve and the fans' anger and disgust.

Push and pull others into inappropriate action. BS cultures stimulate action, any action, over reflection and learning. The more militant owners pulled the others into taking action without reflecting and discovering other responses with less negative results. Many of the players also jumped from stimulus to action with no interrupt for central processing in their brains. Those players with reservations were pushed into the strike by BS group dynamics.

Overdo the notion of ready, fire, aim. Doing is more important than planning in a BS organizational culture. The reactions of the players could have been anticipated by the owners and the resolve of the owners could have been factored into the players' decisions. Both the players and owners could have forecast the anger and disgust of the fans. True to the nature of a BS organization, neither side thought and both sides acted prematurely and immaturely without anticipating the consequences of their action.

Learning Organizations

The upper right quadrant of the R-factor model is the exclusive residence of people who have the ability to grow and learn from their experience. This real estate is also highly prized by organizations. The basic R-learning response of engaging and growing results in organizational cultures with a readiness to learn and a capacity to change. This is a combination that will result in a significant competitive advantage and ensure any organization's survival.

Learning organizations have been the subject of an increasing amount of attention in both the academic and popular press. Due to abstraction and reification, some of this information is difficult for the practitioner to use. Two keys that help unlock a better understanding of organizational learning lie in words found in much of this literature: *collective* and *process*. Learning takes place during interaction with others at the small-group, department, and organizational level. It can involve creative techniques such as large-system interventions that get the whole system in the room (Bunker and Alban, 1992), or it can occur in a small-group setting.

In *The Organizational Learning Cycle: How We Can Learn Collectively* (1994), Nancy Dixon does an effective job of demystifying organizational learning and putting it in an operational context for the working leader. She makes the distinction between learning as a fixed activity (noun) and as an interactive process (verb): "The second way the term 'learning' is used is as a verb. . . . At the collective level we might use the term 'learning' as a process to ask, 'What do we need to do to be able to correct our mistakes better as we go along?' . . . Organizational learning . . . is the processes the organization employs to gain new understanding or to correct the current understanding; it is not the accumulated knowledge of the organization" (p. 6).

In his work on organizational learning, Senge (1990, pp. 5–10), outlines five disciplines that characterize a learning organization: systems thinking, personal mastery, mental models, shared vision, and team learning. Dixon (1995, p. 2) postulates four competencies for learning organizations: stimulating innovation, applying lessons learned, implementing change, and challenging assumptions. We will now look at how some of these organizational level disciplines and competencies relate to the four learning responses in the R-Factor model.

Learning Responses

Pay attention to the how of learning. Residents of the learning quadrant, individual or organizational, seek to understand what they learned and how they learned it. They are conscious of their learning process and are passionate in communicating both the what and the how of their learnings. Dixon conceptualizes this as "Applying Lessons Learned." While Senge (1990, p. 238), calls the process *team learning* and encourages the use of dialogue to facilitate it, Dixon emphasizes the communications process when she writes

(1995, p. 5), "Organizations need competence in capturing what has been learned from their experience. . . . If a unit has been successful at a critical objective, that success needs to be captured in a form that others can understand and use. If a unit has tried something and failed, it is important to understand why that failure happened so that it doesn't have to be repeated."

Tap the power of positive doing. As discussed in Chapter Five, the basic individual learning response pattern involves engaging (finding ways to deal productively with change) and growing (learning how to learn and increasing one's reservoir of behavioral options). Learning organizations also engage and find positive responses to the new reality. This active process of positive doing is a cornerstone of systems thinking and underlies Senge's other four disciplines. Dixon (1995, p. 7) frames this action orientation as an organizational competency of "implementing change." She writes, "In these times of fast-paced change organizations need to be able to quickly respond with new strategic direction. . . . Organizations need competence in making rapid change."

Solve problems, don't place personal blame. Learning organizations find ways to blame the system and not the individual. This is a basic tenet of the quality movement. Dixon (1995, p. 8) sees learning from failures as key to stimulating innovation. "Innovation often means trial and error learning. Organizations are often more tolerant of the trial than the errors—but we learn from both." If organizations are to develop the creative responses necessary to compete in the new reality they need to develop learning cultures that focus on the system and not the individual. Amabile and Conti (1995, p. 2) point out that organizational impediments to creativity include "internal political problems, harsh criticism of new ideas, destructive internal competition, an avoidance of risk, and an overemphasis on the status quo."

Accept short-term setbacks for long-term gain. Just as the learning individual is able to accept a short-term decrement in performance in anticipation of a long-term improvement, the learning organization is able to resist the seduction of short-term thinking. This requires the courage and discipline to stay in a painful situation long enough to avoid treating the symptom while allowing the disease to continue its systemic growth. Senge (1990, p. 60) calls such symptom treatment *low-leverage interventions:* "Low-leverage interventions would be much less alluring if it were not for the fact that many actually work in the short term. . . . Compensating feedback usually involves a delay, a time lag between the short-term benefit and the long-term disbenefit."

Learning organizations need to develop cultures that allow them to resist one-dimensional analysis and individual prescriptive responses. Many organizational leaders—reared in a culture that emphasized individual accountability and personal decision making—find this a very difficult experience, running against the grain of everything they have learned. Difficult though it may be, withholding individual analysis and problem solving while taking sufficient time to allow issues to be aired in the collective is the essence of leadership in a learning organization. This is a frightening process for managers reared in individual accountability, but necessary if organizational learning is to take place. Dixon (1995, p. 6) writes, "It is a basic tenet of systems theory that heterogeneity produces energy whereas homogeneity leads to entropy. We need competence in allowing the contrary view to emerge, raising the objections (reasonable and unreasonable alike), and giving voice to our fears and our hopes. The collective learns when it has available to it *all* of the information about the issue—not just the politically correct view."

Assessing Organizational R-Types: Perspective and Observations

Just as individuals develop behavior patterns that cause them to respond to change and transitions in certain predictable ways, organizations also tend to develop norms and values that predispose them to one of the four response patterns. The struggle to move toward more relevant and adaptive responses is waged at both the individual and the systems level. It is a symbiotic relationship: the system provides the contextual background for individual learning and growth, and it requires individual learners to facilitate the collective learning that is the mark of the learning organization. The journey to the upper right quadrant is key to breaking free. Find or develop individuals comfortable with change who have learned how to learn and let them work in organizational systems with the capacity for collective problem solving and learning—that is the formula for organizational productivity and individual growth.

Assessing R-types at either the individual or organizational level is by no means an exact science and care must be taken in labeling. However, viewing organizations through the lenses of the four R-types provides a very valuable perspective in mapping out the terrain for cultural change efforts geared toward moving the system toward collective learning. Evaluating organizational R-types serves another important function: it can, as outlined in the next chapter, serve as a frame of reference for assessing the relationship between the individual response type and that of the organization. From the individual perspective, understanding and taking action in regard to this fit can be an important stimulus toward breaking free and moving toward the productive and exciting life of a learner. For organizations, awareness of the match between employee and system is an important first step for moving both toward the freedom and creativity of the learning response.

Facilitating the Learning Response

R-factor awareness is not a license to label or stereotype; getting a fix on either an individual's or an organization's R-type is more of an art than a science. Literal interpretation, uninformed judging, forming artificial limits and developmental barriers, and using R-type generalizations as an excuse for not doing individual assessment is never appropriate. Kroeger and Thuesen's warning in regard to misuse of the Myers-Briggs Type Indicator (1988) is also appropriate for R-factor usage:

> Type watching is only an explanation. It is never an excuse. We can't emphasize this enough. We've seen it happen among both neophyte and experienced Type-watchers. One person will say, "Gee, it doesn't matter if I'm late, because I'm a Perceiver and P's are always late." Or, "There's no need to tell him how I'm feeling because he's a Thinker and probably wouldn't understand any-way." Suffice it to say, this is no way to further under-standing and communication among people [pp. 73–74].

Charlie's Cult: An Example of Overenthusiasm

The downside of unexamined enthusiastic stereotyping was made clear to me when I worked with Charlie and his staff. Charlie heads a major business unit in a public utility. Charlie and his team were mostly engineers and some, like Charlie, had gone on to secure MBA degrees. They were an extremely positive and hardworking group. They reflected their organization's culture and their own training—that is, they were predisposed to find specific and concrete solutions to abstract and shifting problems. They were very dedicated managers, working hard to become leaders in an organization that was having a wrenching time moving from the old to the new reality.

The Clue: $D = Re^3$

There are certain organizations that get unusually excited—often carried away—by slogans, labels, and formulas. Charlie's group of optimistic engineers was at the top of the class. I got my first inkling of this trait when, during our initial discussion, I put my predictive formula for formerly regulated industries: $D = Re^3$, on a sheet of newsprint. It was meant to stimulate a discussion in regard to my belief that D (deregulation), inevitably leads to the three Re's: (Reengineering, Reorganization, and Restructuring). Another client (not Charlie) once added a fourth Re for many of the people in his organization: Retirement!

Charlie and his staff resonated to the $D = Re^3$ formula. We spent the entire day discussing the three Re's in their business unit, which was not unusual. What was unique about the group was their sheer enthusiasm for the formula itself. One of their after-meeting action items was to have a number of placards designed featuring the formula. They planned on keeping one for themselves for display in their offices and passing others out to their respective staffs.

The Cult

The second time I visited Charlie's group, we used the R-factor as a way to look at their organization's way of coping with the transition they were going through. Again, I was struck by their attachment to labels. The degree of this attachment became clear to me when I returned for a third visit some months later. The day started with a breakfast meeting with Charlie and a new, recently transferred member of his staff.

"I'd like you to meet Jane," he said over coffee. "She's new to my staff and is really going to be helpful, she is a genuine learner. I don't know how she survived in her past organization, her boss was a BSer and we all know that division is entrenched and is rapidly slipping into overwhelmed status."

It was obvious that Jane didn't have the code for this language, and Charlie spent the rest of our breakfast drawing the R-factor model on a napkin. When he told me that Jane was not yet "R-type literate," I ordered some more coffee. It was becoming apparent that it was going to be a very long day!

We met that morning with Charlie's extended staff. The group included the new cross-functional transition team that the group had decided to form during our last meeting. For the first two hours I heard that Charlie's boss was a reformed BSer, that when they selected the transition team they put in a few entrenched, but loaded it with learners. I heard jokes and jibes as in, "Sure, it may look that way to you, but you're overwhelmed!" or, "That whole group that works for you is terminally entrenched, they're never going to change!" Just before the break, I again heard the term *R-type literate*. This time it was applied to another group in the organization who were not enlightened. It was clear to me, as we took a break, that Charlie had created a cult, complete with initiation rites and insider-outsider language barriers.

Deprogramming

It took a few more sessions, both with Charlie individually and with the team, but we deprogrammed the cult out of the group. They still use the R-factor model, but have come to better understand that, like any model, it is only a tool to facilitate communication and understanding; it is an abstraction, not reality.

Charlie's short-lived mini cult demonstrates that tools are means, not ends. It is a propensity of the technically and quantitatively educated such as Charlie and his staff to become enamored with technique and lose sight of desired outcomes. This tendency is discussed by Barrett in his aptly titled book, *The Illusion of Technique*, (1978, p. 88) when he writes, "Technique has no meaning apart from some informing vision."

The Right Way to Use Models

Organizational systems and the humans that populate them are too complex for rote labeling or sophomoric stereotyping. One characteristic of open systems is the principle of *equifinality* (Katz and Kahn, 1966, pp. 25–26). Equifinality states that systems can start at different points and use different means, yet arrive at the same end point. Said more plainly, there are many ways to skin a cat. In complex systems, models are necessary ways of abstracting reality—but they never *are* reality. Real life is much too complex and diverse to ever fit precisely into the confines of a theory or model. Care must be taken with any model to minimize labeling, projection, and artificial differentiation between those who know the jargon and those who don't.

Given these cautions, there are many positive aspects of models in general, and the R-factor model in particular. The best models create a language that facilitates a common frame of reference to better deal with complexity. Without models that distill reality and allow us to generalize, meaningful discussion—let alone informative dialogue—would be very difficult. When working with organizational leaders, one of my first questions is to ask them to explain their model of change and transition. If, as is the case with a fair number of them, they say they don't have a model, I help them discover that they really do, although they may have difficulty in articulating it. We all have mental models from which we operate and the more explicit we can make them the better we are able to communicate. The advantage of prepackaged models—such as the Myers-Briggs personality type, the Bridges (1980) change process of beginnings, endings, and neutral zones, or my R-factor model of differential response to transitions—is that they offer a common language. In prepackaged models, this language helps facilitate communication and analysis across and within many organizational systems.

Home Rooms and Migration Patterns

Our location in the R-factor model is dynamic: we can all, if we are honest, remember spending time in all four boxes. One harassed and busy executive recently commented that he traveled through all four boxes and back again during the first hour he was at the office. But we have a very strong tendency to spend most of our time in one of the boxes, which functions as a type of home room. We may stray, but until we make a permanent migration we almost always come back.

There seem to be four migration patterns: one horizontal, one vertical, and two diagonal. There is a great deal of variance in the amount of traffic and some routes are mostly one-way. Some roads are smooth and well traveled, such as the route between the entrenched and overwhelmed. Others, such as the trail between the residences of the BSers and the entrenched are rough and bumpy. Although movement can occur between any of the boxes there are four primary patterns.

The Entrenched-Overwhelmed Expressway

This route has the most traffic. There is a steady flow of overwhelmed employees moving north. They have found a way to deal with at least the most debilitating aspects of their stress; have discovered the ability to change, uncomfortable though it may be; and are able to perform useful work, albeit of an entrenched variety. In the other lane, heading south, are entrenched employees who are unable to hang on. They have lost their ability to change, are withdrawing from facing their problems, and are avoiding the necessary adjustment. There is an equal amount of traffic in the southbound lane.

The Entrenched-Learner Country Road

This is a paved two-lane road. It carries less traffic than the expressway and most of it is heading east toward the land of the learner. The drivers are smiling because they are unstuck and moving in the right direction. This eastbound traffic is made up of formerly entrenched employees who are learning new, more relevant coping patterns, and are developing more comfort with change with every mile they drive. There is an occasional car heading west. The drivers are not smiling and are spending a lot of time looking in their rear-view mirrors. The westbounders are learners who have burned out and are temporarily retreating into the fortress of the entrenched. They aren't pulling trailers and don't have much luggage. They plan on returning soon.

The BS-Entrenched Trail

This is a winding trail, leading out of the land of the BSer, across the back country in a northwesterly direction. It's a rough ride and a four-wheel-drive vehicle is the best bet. There is not a lot of traffic, but there are a few vehicles on the road every day. Although there is a very rare driver heading southeast, this is essentially a one-way trail toward the land of the entrenched. Most of the drivers are BSers of the uninformed optimist variety. Once the bubble has been burst, they drive nonstop to the residence of the entrenched. For them, it's a painful drive, but the entrenched life is a big step forward. It's a much more difficult journey for those few hard-core BSers that gain the insight necessary to take it. The price of self-understanding is often anger and disillusionment. Thus, they head for the land of the entrenched with the requisite emotions. There is something very interesting about the former BSers who make this journey. Perhaps it's the arrogance and insensitivity that made them BSers in the first place, but one has to admire their self-reliance and grit. Almost none of them travel to the land of the overwhelmed.

The Learner-Overwhelmed Orienteering Course

This is a one-way trek from the land of the learner in a southwesterly direction toward the residence of the overwhelmed. It isn't actually a trail at all. Those few who attempt it take maps and a compass and set off on foot. The trekkers are made up of a special category called overwhelmed learners. They suffer from a severe case of the learner's disease—burnout. Those with mild cases travel the entrenched-learner country road and, after a short retreat performing routine work, return. Those with more severe cases drop out and trek into the wilderness. Most of them don't complete the voyage and eventually return. A few, however, don't come back.

R-Factor Worksheets

This section introduces analytical tools in the form of worksheets and rating processes that can help discover both organizational and individual response patterns. But first, a couple of words: one of caution and the other of encouragement.

The word of caution: these are worksheets and not psychometric instruments. They have not been proven either valid or reliable in a scientific sense. Not that their validity and reliability have been disproved, but that's not the point. In this format, they are intended to be used as worksheets and not as psychometrically proven feedback instruments.

The word of encouragement: these worksheets can be extremely helpful and their application is only limited by the creativity of the practitioner. One primary value of the organizational version of the worksheet and rating form is to facilitate communication. Users are encouraged to use both dialogue and skillful discussion in this process.

Skillful discussion implies just that: a discussion that emphasizes listening and mutual learning, but with an outcome goal. Dialogue is a process of collective learning, which is itself the outcome goal. These are two very powerful processes and of great importance to learning. Rick Ross (1994) diagrams a continuum of interaction from "raw debate" to "polite discussion" to "skillful discussion" and finally to dialogue. He differentiates between skillful discussion and dialogue as follows:

> In skillful discussion the team intends to come to some sort of closure—either to make a decision, reach agreement, or identify priorities. Along the way, the team may explore new issues and build some deeper meaning among the members. But their intent involves convergent thinking.
>
> In dialogue the intention is exploration, discovery, and insight. Along that path, the group may in fact sometimes come to a meeting of the minds and reach some agreement—but that isn't their primary purpose in coming together [p. 386].

Dialogue is the language of learning organizations. Without it, true collective learning does not happen. The organizational version of these worksheets and rating processes provides some very interesting data for teams and other groups of employees to use as input to a dialogue. The dialogue process is defined by Isaacs (1994):

> It is based on the principle that conception and implementation are intimately linked, with a core of common meaning. During the dialogue process, people learn how to think together—not just in the sense of analyzing a shared problem or creating new pieces of shared knowledge, but in the sense of occupying a collective sensibility, in which the thoughts, emotions and resulting actions belong not to one individual, but to all of them together [p. 358].

Organizational Response Analysis

What is found in Exhibit 7.1 is a process to gather information about perceptions of organizational response patterns. It uses the

Exhibit 7.1. Organizational R-Factor Analysis.

This worksheet provides a process for you to structure your perceptions of how your organization is responding to change along four dimensions: how people are feeling, how the organization reacts to transitions, how the organization learns, and the type of leadership needed to assure survival.

Ranking Instructions: Choose a level of analysis such as the entire organization, your division, or your department. Consistently use that level for all four sections. For each section, choose the statement that comes closest to your perception of your organization. Put the letter of that statement in the brackets following "most descriptive." Next, choose the statement that is "least descriptive" of your organization and place that letter in the appropriate brackets. Finally, complete the remaining two choices.

I. How People in This Organization Feel

A.   People in this organization feel powerless and depressed.

B.   People in this organization feel threatened and angry. Many believe that we have lost sight of the past, are forgetting what made us what we are.

C.   Many people in this organization are frustrated with all the complaining and whining. They are ready to take action—to do something—anything!

D.   People in this organization feel in control of their own destiny and, although anxious about the changes, are feeling optimistic and positive. They have faith that the organization can change and create a culture that will lead to a long-term future.

Section I Rankings: *Most descriptive*   (_____)
                      Second most descriptive   (_____)
                      Third most descriptive   (_____)
                      Least descriptive   (_____)

II. How This Organization Reacts to Transitions

A.   This organization has norms and values that don't allow us to confront the real issues. We withdraw and retreat into safe activities.

B.   This organization has many communication processes that emphasize the need to change but it is all talk. We can't seem to make it happen.

Exhibit 7.1. Organizational R-Factor Analysis, Cont'd.

C.   This organization values slogans, gimmicks, and unrealistic, rote optimism.

D.   This organization understands the necessity of transition and seeks positive ways to deal with change.

Section II Rankings: *Most descriptive*   (_____)
                       Second most descriptive   (_____)
                       Third most descriptive   (_____)
                       Least descriptive   (_____)

III. How This Organization Learns

A.   This organization has norms and values that cause it to block and avoid the necessary learning.

B.   This organization works very hard at previously successful problem-solving processes that are of dubious value to our current or future needs.

C.   This organization values action and activity over reflection and diagnosis. Doing something is better than investing the time and energy necessary to learn something.

D.   This organization has the discipline and patience to engage with problems at the basic, systemic level. We blame systems, not people.

Section III Rankings: *Most descriptive*   (_____)
                        Second most descriptive   (_____)
                        Third most descriptive   (_____)
                        Least descriptive   (_____)

IV. Type of Leadership This Organization Needs to Assure Survival

A.   This organization needs leadership that will end our victim mentality. We need leaders to help build a culture that restores confidence that we are in charge of our own future.

B.   This organization needs a leadership process that will encourage, support, and stimulate moving away from the comfortable but unproductive old to a new and more relevant culture.

C.   This organization needs a leadership process that facilitates reflection and learning, and eliminates premature and unconditional action.

Exhibit 7.1. Organizational R-Factor Analysis, Cont'd.

D.   This organization needs leaders who will continue to develop a learning culture by allowing collective learning to replace individual decision making, and allowing dialogue to supplant arbitrariness.

Section IV Rankings: *Most descriptive*   (_____)

                        Second most descriptive   (_____)

                        Third most descriptive   (_____)

                        Least descriptive   (_____)

---

familiar categories of overwhelmed, entrenched, and BSer. The learning response is framed in leadership behavior that will facilitate the learning appropriate to the organization's R-type.

Organizational R-Factor Worksheet: Scoring and Analysis

What follows in Exhibit 7.2 is a suggested three-step process for analyzing the results of the organizational R-factor worksheet ranking process. It is not intended to be either exhaustive or prescriptive, but only to show one example of how this data may be used.

Enter the most descriptive and least descriptive R-type for each section. All letter A's represent the overwhelmed response pattern, B's represent an entrenched response, C's are BS responses, and D's equate to a learning response.

Analyze the second and third most descriptive responses for any trends. This, combined with the most descriptive–least descriptive comparison, and any differences between the four sections will provide a great deal of data on your perception of the level of the organization you chose to examine. Note that "Leadership Needs" has to do with the focus and activity of leadership as opposed to describing the response pattern of the organization's leaders.

Use the data in three ways: to facilitate dialogues among organizational stakeholders, to deepen your own understanding of

Exhibit 7.2. Organizational R-Type Preferences.

	Most Descriptive	Least Descriptive
Feelings	(_____)	(_____)
Transition reaction	(_____)	(_____)
Learning pattern	(_____)	(_____)
Leadership needs	(_____)	(_____)

the organizational culture, and to assess the fit between your personal response types and those of the organization. Here are some examples:

- Have others complete the same level of analysis and compare the results. This provides good data for team-building sessions and for comparison between organizational levels and different functions. This is particularly valuable in discovering differences in assumptions and perceptions.

- Complete the ranking process at three levels of analysis and compare the results. For example: total organization, division, department.

- Complete the self-analysis worksheet and compare the self- responses to the organizational responses.

Individual Response Analysis

What follows in Exhibit 7.3 is a process to gather information in regard to self-perceptions of individual response patterns. As was the case with the organizational version, this self-analysis is structured around the overwhelmed, entrenched, and BS response categories. The learning response is framed in terms of desired leadership behavior that will facilitate the learning appropriate to the self-perceived R-type.

Exhibit 7.3. Individual R-Type Analysis.

This worksheet provides a process for you to structure your self-perceptions of how you are personally responding to change along four dimensions: how you are feeling, how you react to transitions, how you are functioning as a learner, and the type of leadership you need to be a successful survivor.

Ranking Instructions: For each section, choose the statement that comes closest to the way you honestly see yourself. Put the letter of that statement in the brackets following "most descriptive." Next, choose the statement that is "least descriptive" of the way you see yourself and place that letter in the appropriate brackets. Finally, complete the remaining two choices.

I. How I Feel

A.   I feel anxious, powerless, and depressed. I'm not in charge of my own destiny and I don't know what to do about it.

B.   I'm angry and frustrated. I feel my past skills are not valued in the new organization. I feel discounted.

C.   I feel absolutely confident of my ability to handle any aspect of the new reality. I'm impatient with all the whining and intellectualizing. We need to get on with it!

D.   I feel challenged, stretched, and optimistic.

Section I Rankings:	*Most descriptive*	(_____)
	Second most descriptive	(_____)
	Third most descriptive	(_____)
	Least descriptive	(_____)

II. How I'm Reacting to the Transition

A.   I'm keeping my head down and looking for a safe job. My strategy is to find a place to hide: a refuge where I can wait it out until things get back to normal.

B.   I'm trying to mask and contain my anger but it keeps slipping out. I understand the need to change in my head, but not in my heart. That's why I give myself and others mixed signals.

Exhibit 7.3. Individual R-Type Analysis, Cont'd.

C.   I refuse to let myself and others spend any time on all this emotionalism and negative thinking. There is nothing wrong with this organization that a little old-fashioned enthusiasm and energy won't fix. I'm pushing and pulling people into action even if they resist.

D.   I understand the necessity of change and I'm keeping myself up and finding ways to help others cope and move forward.

Section II Rankings: *Most descriptive*   (_____)
                        Second most descriptive   (_____)
                        Third most descriptive   (_____)
                        Least descriptive   (_____)

III. How I'm Functioning as a Learner

A.   I'm withdrawing and am unable to learn. My stress and anxiety have caused me to shut down.

B.   I'm working very hard but seem to be spinning my wheels. I know this is not the answer but I don't know what else to do. Hard work and compliance with the organizational culture always seemed to work in the past.

C.   I'm not into learning, I'm into doing. We are not going to learn our way out of our problems, we need to get out there and work our way out.

D.   I'm learning how to deal with the root problems and not just the symptoms. I'm helping the organization and myself. It is stressful, but it's also exciting and personally developmental.

Section III Rankings: *Most descriptive*   (_____)
                         Second most descriptive   (_____)
                         Third most descriptive   (_____)
                         Least descriptive   (_____)

IV. The Type of Leadership I Need to Be a Successful Survivor

A.   I need a leader who will give me help in dealing with my stress, fear, and anxiety.

Exhibit 7.3. Individual R-Type Analysis, Cont'd.

B.   I need a leader who will give me feedback and support so I can drop old and previously successful behavior patterns that are not relevant in today's organization.

C.   I need a leader who will give me developmental assignments that push me into understanding the depth and breadth of the underlying issues.

D.   I need a leader who will give me assignments with high organizational impact. I need feedback and support so that I don't burn out by trying to be all things to all people.

Section IV Rankings: *Most descriptive*   (_____)
                          Second most descriptive (_____)
                          Third most descriptive   (_____)
                          Least descriptive   (_____)

Individual R-Factor Worksheet: Scoring and Analysis

What follows in Exhibit 7.4 is a suggested process of analyzing the results of the self-evaluation and ranking process. As was the case with the organizational version, it is not intended to be the one true way, but only to show an example of how this data may be used.

Enter the most descriptive and least descriptive R-type for each section. All letter A's represent the overwhelmed response pattern, B's represent an entrenched response, C's are BS responses, and D's equate to a learning response.

Analyze the second and third most descriptive responses for any trends. This, combined with the most descriptive–least descriptive comparison and any differences between the four sections, will provide a great deal of information on how you perceive your own response patterns. Note that "Leadership Needs" has to do with the type of leadership you need to be a successful survivor, not your own leadership style.

Exhibit 7.4. Individual R-Type Preferences.

	Most Descriptive	Least Descriptive
Feelings	(_____)	(_____)
Transition reaction	(_____)	(_____)
Learning pattern	(_____)	(_____)
Leadership needs	(_____)	(_____)

This data can be used to deepen your insight, as a structure for feedback, or as an impetus for taking action. Here are some ideas:

- An honest self-analysis can serve as a mirror to discover your personal response patterns. This does not require sharing or discussion to serve as a stimulus for self-reflection.

- Although this is a self-analysis tool and not intended to be a feedback instrument, you can ask someone you trust enough to be honest with you to fill out the rating form based on their observations. You can also simply share your response pattern and ask for feedback. This can be a very powerful learning experience.

- It can be a catalyst for goal setting and action planning. Outcomes could range from asking your boss for the type of leadership you need to deciding to leave the organization.

- You can complete the organizational worksheet and compare the self-responses to the organizational responses.

Self–System Connection

Another interesting analytical frame involves a comparison of individual "most descriptive" and "least descriptive" responses to those of the organization. This is easily done by extrapolating the data from the organizational and individual R-factor worksheets. These results can then be summarized with the help of Exhibit 7.5.

This information can be analyzed in many different ways: the fit between the individual and the organization, the most and least frequently occurring response for self and system, and the overall patterns—including any section that differs from the pattern. The data can be used as a stimulus for self-reflection and planning without sharing with anyone. It is not designed and should not be used as a feedback instrument. If, however, the respondent wants to check out self-perceptions and organizational perceptions with a trusted associate familiar enough to generate valid data, this consultation can lead to deeper insight.

Fits, Misfits, and Strategies

Using one primary response type for individuals and organizations produces sixteen potential combinations. The good news, the bad news, and a suggested strategy for each of these connections is summarized in Table 7.1 and outlined in this section.

Exhibit 7.5. Self–System R-Type Comparisons.

| | Organization | | Self | |
	Most	Least	Most	Least
Feelings	(_____)	(_____)	(_____)	(_____)
Transition reaction	(_____)	(_____)	(_____)	(_____)
Learning pattern	(_____)	(_____)	(_____)	(_____)
Leadership needs	(_____)	(_____)	(_____)	(_____)

Table 7.1. Self–System Response Connections.

Individual \ Organization	Overwhelmed	Entrenched	BS	Learning
Overwhelmed	*Good News:* You are among friends. *Bad News:* You are among the wrong friends. *Strategy:* Escape/symptom relief.	*Good News:* You have the ability to get caught up in "doing something." *Bad News:* No opportunity for symptom relief. *Strategy:* Connect with the work/seek outside symptom relief.	*Good News:* You are getting a sense of direction. *Bad News:* There is a high probability it may be the wrong direction. *Strategy:* Resist being swept away/find symptom relief outside organization.	*Good News:* The learning organization is the best place to be. *Bad News:* If you are too far gone the system will reject you. *Strategy:* Reach out/accept help.
Entrenched	*Good News:* Unlike the organization, you have the ability to learn and change. *Bad News:* The organization doesn't support your ability to learn and change. *Strategy:* Take the risk of new behavior.	*Good News:* Both you and your organization have the ability to learn and change. *Bad News:* An entrenched employee in an entrenched organization is hard to budge. *Strategy:* Find some slack time/take baby steps.	*Good News:* Your rigidity provides a sense of direction. *Bad News:* The swashbuckling culture may cause you to become further entrenched. *Strategy:* Seriously consider leaving.	*Good News:* The learning culture will pull you out of your fortress and facilitate learning. *Bad News:* If you are truly entrenched, the system will reject you. *Strategy:* Trust the process,let go.
BS	*Good News:* You will have lots of influence. *Bad News:* You may take the organization the wrong way fast. *Strategy:* Use the non-threatening environment to seek feedback.	*Good News:* The entrenched culture gives you much needed boundaries. *Bad News:* The culture will not facilitate the necessary self-awareness. *Strategy:* Stay with the pain/learn how to change.	*Good News:* No organizational impediments for ready, fire, aim behavior. *Bad News:* Long-term organizational prognosis not good. *Strategy:* Seek feedback/become self-aware.	*Good News:* Opportunity to gain much needed feedback. *Bad News:* You are in an up or out situation. *Strategy:* Move against the grain/don't sabotage yourself.
Learner	*Good News:* Multiple opportunities to serve. *Bad News:* Too many needy people. *Strategy:* Have a good reason to stay/beware of burnout.	*Good News:* Opportunity to make a major impact. *Bad News:* Frustrating environment. *Strategy:* Coach and guide/don't push too hard.	*Good News:* You have the relevant skills to help. *Bad News:* Beware of frustration and burnout. *Strategy:* Decide if you really want to stay/network with other learners.	*Good News:* Marriage made in heaven. *Bad News:* Could overdose on a good thing. *Strategy:* Set limits/avoid burnout.

The Four Fits

Overwhelmed-Overwhelmed. The overwhelmed person working in an overwhelmed organization is not a pretty sight. It's akin to a leper connecting with a leper colony.

- *The Good News:* If you are an overwhelmed employee working in an overwhelmed organization, the good news is you are among friends in a familiar environment.

- *The Bad News:* The bad news is that you are among the wrong friends in an environment that, although familiar, is toxic to your long-term survival.

- *The Strategy:* There are two steps:

    Like all those with R-overwhelmed behavior you need symptom relief. Chances are you are not going to get that from an overwhelmed organization, so you need to seek relief from your fear, anxiety, and depression outside the organization.

    The broader strategy is to escape. An overwhelmed employee working in an overwhelmed organization has a very slim chance of survival. Escape can either involve finding a less overwhelmed part of your current organization, leaving the organization entirely, or finding a learner as a coach and a mentor who will help you escape on a psychological level.

Entrenched-Entrenched. The entrenched employee working in an entrenched organization is stuck in a stuck organization. It gives new meaning to the concept of a double bind!

- *The Good News:* You and your organization have one good connection; you both have the ability to learn and change.

- *The Bad News:* It's much harder for the entrenched employee stuck in an entrenched organization to develop the courage to take the necessary baby steps toward the learning box.

- *The Strategy:* Success requires a two-pronged approach:

  Find some slack time. Difficult though it may be, resist the action frenzy of working increasingly harder on increasingly irrelevant things that are likely to be occurring in your organization.

  Use your extra time to learn. Find a way, probably away from your job and in a place like a community agency or other volunteer organization, to rebuild your risk-taking ability and to practice new, more adaptive behavior. Reformed entrenched employees who have found ways to demonstrate new and more relevant response patterns have done very well in entrenched systems. They stand out and are often the stimulus for others to take the necessary risks. They move into the land of the learner.

BS-BS. The BS employee working in a BS organizational culture is in hog heaven—and it often smells that way to an outsider.

- *The Good News:* If you are a BS employee in a BS organization, you are working in a system that is congruent with your basic behavior pattern: there will be no organizational impediments to your basic ready, fire, aim pattern. You can move directly from stimulus to response with no processing time in your brain.

- *The Bad News:* The long-term prognosis for BS organizations is not very good, and since learners are few and far between in these organizations, there is a severe scarcity of people who can give you the valid feedback you need.

- *The Strategy:* The basic strategy is to become more self-aware. This is much easier said than done for anyone, and is very difficult for the hard-core BSer. Structured, instrumented feedback helps, particularly if it is delivered by a professional and if the recipient finds a way to accept it.

Learner–Learning Organization. This is a marriage made in heaven! A person who has learned how to learn working in an organizational system that has found a way to do its own collective learning is in the best of all possible worlds.

- *The Good News:* If you are a learner who is lucky enough to work in a learning organization you are in a win-win partnership situation. Your personal growth and productivity will be maximized, and the organization will thrive and prosper.

- *The Bad News:* You have the propensity to overdose on too much of a good thing.

- *The Strategy:* Avoid the learner's disease—burnout. Set some limits!

The Twelve Misfits

Overwhelmed-Learner. If you are an overwhelmed employee in a learning organization things definitely have the potential to improve. You may feel as though you've fallen overboard, but your organization has attracted and developed many learners. They all have life buoys in their hands and are ready and willing to throw them to you.

- *The Good News:* You may be sinking—but there are lots of lifeguards able to help. If you must be overwhelmed, a learning organization is the best place to be.

- *The Bad News:* The gap may be too wide. If you are too far gone (an outward-bound overwhelmed), the system may reject you. Even the most compassionate learning organizations are involved in a fast-paced and competitive game. High-performance systems have a limited tolerance for bench sitters.

- *The Strategy:* Reach out! You need to meet the system halfway. You can't wallow in your withdrawal and avoidance and expect to be helped. If you expend a little effort you can expect a big payback from the system. If you expend no effort, you will get the same in return.

Learner-Overwhelmed. A learner in an overwhelmed organization is a stranger in a strange, strange land. There are so many opportunities to help and so little time!

- *The Good News:* If you are a learner in an overwhelmed organization, you have multiple opportunities to be of service.

- *The Bad News:* There are needy systems and people all around you. You can't be all things to all people. Unless careful, you could help your way into the category of overwhelmed learner—which is not where you or your organization want you to be.

- *The Strategy:* There are two parts:

  Decide if you want to stay. There are lots of options for a learner out there and you are planting your seeds in some awfully rocky and dry soil.

  If you do decide to stay, set some limits. The learner's disease, burnout, is an ever-present danger.

BS-Overwhelmed. A BSer, particularly an influential manager, in an overwhelmed organization can be the classical bull in a china shop. He will run in circles with a great deal of noise and furor. At the end of the day, there will be much breakage and the organization will continue its downward plunge.

- *The Good News:* If you are a BSer, you will have lots of influence. Overwhelmed organizations collect overwhelmed employees and they are almost all looking for direction.

- *The Bad News:* The bad news for the organization is that the direction received by the self-actualized BSer may take the organization the wrong direction with ever-increasing speed.

- *The Strategy:* Strange though it may seem, overwhelmed organizational cultures have provided learning environments for some BS employees. Everyone is so down that there is no competition. The hard-core BSer can proceed unchecked. The nonthreatening environment with no competition seems to make learning easier for some BSers. They hear feedback more easily and seem to have an easier time moving toward self-awareness. This, unfortunately, does not happen with regularity, and the core strategic challenge for all BSers remains: the need to gain self-insight.

Overwhelmed-BS. If you are an overwhelmed employee in a BS organizational culture, welcome to the parade of lemmings: the cliff is just ahead! You may feel good about the direction you are going, but don't look down.

- *The Good News:* You are getting a sense of direction.

- *The Bad News:* It may not be where you or the organization need to go. You are also probably feeling discounted: BSers have no tolerance for your very real feelings of fear, anxiety, and depression.

- *The Strategy:* There are two things you can do:

  Resist going to Abilene. (This refers to Harvey's classic tale [1988] of publicly colluding to do something that individually no one wants to do.) Comforting though it may feel for a strong person to be giving you the feeling that things are under control, you can't afford to believe it.

  Find a way, almost certainly outside the BS organization, to deal with your survivor guilt. You won't get anywhere with those rocks in your pack.

Entrenched-Overwhelmed. The entrenched employee in an overwhelmed organization is like a passenger on the *Titanic* who refuses to get in a lifeboat. Better to ride a sinking ship to the bottom of the sea than experiment with new behavior!

- *The Good News:* If you are an entrenched employee in a system with an overwhelmed culture, you are at a big advantage. Unlike the organization, you have the ability to learn and change.

- *The Bad News:* You are stuck in a culture that is withdrawing and avoiding the learning necessary to survive.

- *The Strategy:* Get unstuck. Take the risk of changing your behavior. If the organizational culture is indeed overwhelmed, there isn't a lot of risk in taking a risk!

Overwhelmed-Entrenched. The overwhelmed employee in an entrenched culture is like a patient who visits a therapist for help, but spends the appointment time listening to the therapist's problems. The primary need of the overwhelmed employee is symptom relief—and the entrenched culture is incapable of meeting this need. Anger and a death grip on old ways of coping block out any orientation toward empathy.

- *The Good News:* There is some useful work taking place in entrenched organizations and the overwhelmed employee can get caught up in doing something. Doing something is always better than doing nothing and withdrawing, which is a primary characteristic of the overwhelmed response.

- *The Bad News:* The anger and frustration of the entrenched organization does not allow for the symptom relief the overwhelmed employee desperately needs.

- *The Strategy:* If you are an overwhelmed employee in an entrenched organization you have a balancing act between two tasks:

  Connect with the work being done and stop your withdrawal process.

  Don't get totally caught up in the action frenzy. You also have to attend to your basic need: finding a way, probably outside the organization, of dealing with your survivor guilt.

Entrenched-BS. The entrenched employee who resides in a BS organization is locked into perpetuating a culture unable to make the necessary adjustment for long-term survival. Without major changes, BS organizations just aren't up to the task of survival. As they say in the South, "That dawg won't hunt!" Unfortunately, entrenched employees in a BS organization are in a process that involves feeding, training, and taking that dog to the field every day.

- *The Good News:* The entrenched employee's high ability and low comfort with change complements the BS organization's high comfort and low ability. There is a possible accommodation. In some BS organizations, the rigidity and lockstep doggedness of the entrenched are the only things that keep things on track.

- *The Bad News:* The volatility of a BS culture often causes the entrenched employee to hunker further down in the trenches and refuse to take any of the risks necessary to facilitate behavior change.

- *The Strategy:* If you are an entrenched employee in a BS organization, you must first of all decide if it is in your best interest to stay. One of the characteristics of your R-type is reluctance to break out of even nonproductive relationships, so this is a difficult task—but one that needs consideration. If you do decide to stay, your primary need is to develop a more appropriate behavioral repertoire that will help you contribute to the basic task of moving the organization out of its BS orientation. Attempting to move a BS culture is a daunting task, even for the best learners, which is why you need to give serious consideration to leaving. Who knows, in a new environment, you may find it easier to become a learner yourself?

BS-Entrenched. A BS employee trapped in an entrenched organizational culture is like a toothless wolf living among a flock of sheep. He can stir them up and chase them in circles, but when it comes down to it he has no real impact.

- *The Good News:* An entrenched culture puts some needed boundaries around the BS behavior pattern.

- *The Bad News:* The institutionalized anger and dedication to the old ways will not facilitate the self-awareness and learning necessary to break BS response behavior patterns.

- *The Strategy:* If you are a BS employee in an entrenched organization, you are in an extremely frustrating situation. However, from frustration comes learning. Your best strategy is to stay with the pain and begin to emulate the best of entrenched behavior: hard work and focus. Even if it is outdated focus, it is still focus—which you badly need. A second activity involves assimilating the good side of the entrenched culture: the ability to learn and change. If you can learn that and add it to your comfort with change, you have a winning combination.

Entrenched-Learner. An entrenched employee in a learning organization has the potential to make a very positive future. It is similar to the bright child who finally connects with a teacher who recognizes and deals with a previously undiagnosed learning disability.

- *The Good News:* There is a good chance that immersion in a learning culture will pull the entrenched employee out of the fortress and facilitate the necessary personal growth and learning. This has the potential of vastly increasing the employee's organizational relevance and productivity.

- *The Bad News:* A true learning organization is relentless in its pursuit of excellence. It won't tolerate entrenched behavior patterns that get in the way. There is a possibility that the truly entrenched employee, pulled too soon and too fast, will drop out and sink into the overwhelmed category.

- *The Strategy:* If you are an entrenched employee in a learning organization, you need to trust the process. Letting go of the old may be difficult, but you have a lot of support and the system will work for you. You just have to trust enough to let go.

Learner-Entrenched. The learner operating within an entrenched organizational culture has the opportunity to operate as a guide and a coach. It is a scout-leader model, with the learner holding a lantern and guiding the entrenched employees through the dark forest into the light.

- *The Good News:* The learner has the opportunity to make a major impact by acting as a role model and coach.

- *The Bad News:* The entrenched culture is difficult to move—because it is entrenched. Entrenched employees dig their heels in because they, too, are extremely reluctant to change. This truculence can be very frustrating for a learner.

- *The Strategy:* It is a coaching and guiding strategy. Too much direct effort will backfire and the culture will snap back and the people will dig in even deeper.

BS-Learning. This is a shotgun wedding. The BSer will either gain some badly needed self-awareness or will land on the street. There is no halfway house. The learning organization rejects toxic people—that's how it retains its health.

- *The Good News:* There is an opportunity for the BS employee to gain some valuable feedback and to see what a high-performance system is really all about.

- *The Bad News:* It is an up-or-out system, and the hard-core BSer has a very difficult time staying out of character long enough to learn.

- *The Strategy:* It is an against-the-grain strategy. If you are a BS employee working in a learning organization, your challenge is to behave counter to your nature and be open to new learnings. You have a wonderful opportunity to develop some relevant skills and gain some self-awareness. Don't sabotage yourself.

Learner-BS. If you are a learner in a BS organization, you may feel like a peacemaker parachuted into a throng of warring barbarian tribes. They need you to help them stop killing each other and plan a collective future, but it's very difficult to get their attention. You are very much alone.

- *The Good News:* Learners are needed and can help. BS organizations are on a path of self-destruction. The skills, perspectives, and helping orientation of learners offer hope to these unproductive organizational cultures.

- *The Bad News:* Learners are few and far between in organizations with BS cultures. It's hard to be heard and difficult to make an impact. Frustration and burnout await those who want to push too far, too fast.

- *The Strategy:* Once again, there are two options:

    Decide if you really want to stay. There are many interesting opportunities for learners out there. A BS organizational culture is an alien world. Why stay?

    If you do stay, approach your job as though you were a missionary. Stay connected to the home church: network with other learners outside the organization.

A few strategic conversions and the development of
a supportive infrastructure represents a significant
contribution.

Facilitating the Learning Response: Perspective and Observations

R-factor analysis helps develop the learning response in both individual employees and organizational systems. The assessment and rating system outlined in this chapter provides a mechanism for speculating as to organizational R-type, an individual self-assessment, and a process for comparing self with system.

The purpose of these speculations and ratings is not to apply a psychometrically valid and reliable measurement system, but rather to gather data (opinions, speculations, and perceptions) as input for individual reflection and collective dialogue. The primary value of R-type speculation is not entertainment or categorizing organizations or people, it is furthering the development of learning organizations and learning employees and facilitating the learning response.

This learning response at both the individual and organizational level is the key to unlocking individual potential and organizational productivity. As we shall explore in the next section, it is the prerequisite for breaking free.

Part IV

Learning to Learn

8

Liberation Leadership

Organizational leaders play a key role in helping individuals and organizations break free from the old reality. They facilitate the movement from overwhelmed, entrenched, and BS response patterns to the learning response. They are, to coin a word, the *potkeepers* of the new glue, assuring the adhesive is fresh and relevant. This leadership role is very different from that played in the past. I call it *liberation leadership* because it facilitates the development of the learning response in both individuals and organizations. This learning response frees people to invest their energy in psychically nurturing work that facilitates increased organizational productivity.

Attempting to define leadership has always been a bit like defining love, truth, or justice: the definition varies by context and says as much about the values and perspective of the person doing the defining as it adds to any kind of universal explanation. In his comprehensive work on leadership definitions and practice, Joseph Rost (1991, p. 6) expresses his frustration with this reality, "Without an agreed-upon definition, all kinds of activities, processes, and persons are labeled as leadership by both scholars and practitioners. . . . The worst part of the present situation is that many scholars do not see this inability to agree upon a definition of leadership as a problem."

I find myself in the camp of those who don't get overly excited by the lack of an agreed definition. I worry more about the stultifying effects of rigid boundaries. It is, however, clear that there is a basic change from the type of leadership that fit the old paradigm to that of the new reality. This change can be seen by comparing what Rost calls the industrial paradigm of leadership with his own definition.

Rost's industrial paradigm: "a fundamental understanding of leadership that is rational, management oriented, male, technocratic, quantitative, goal dominated, cost-benefit driven, personalistic, hierarchical, short-term, pragmatic, and materialistic" (p. 94).

Rost's own definition: "Leadership is an influence relationship among leaders and followers who intend real changes that reflect their mutual purposes" (p. 102).

Liberation leadership fits Rost's definition; it stimulates mutual learning and it recognizes that, in the new paradigm, commitment is fostered by influence and not coercion, and that real change is necessary for individuals and organizations to break free. This definition does not exclude top management. The mutuality of liberation leadership requires that we do not play the deification game. We can no longer afford to put our top leaders on pedestals, only to knock them off when things go wrong. We need to stop the collusive process of making our top managers act like cowboys.

Of Cowboys and Leaders

In mellifluous tones, Willie Nelson tells us that his "heroes have always been cowboys," and, in reminding us that "they still are, it seems," approaches the way many of us persist in seeing top managers.

Cowboys: macho, self-reliant, clearly differentiated good guys in a world where the divisions are easy. Larger-than-life characters who, when we really think about it, seem shallow and contrived, somehow unreal, without the requisite frailties that make us human.

I see the classic Clint Eastwood spaghetti Western where the hero rides into town and, amidst interspersions of weird music and endless camera panning, wipes out dozens of bad guys while hardly breaking a sweat himself. In the end, he rides away into the mist. Interesting guy, but would I want him for a neighbor? For sure, not as a boss or someone to help build a learning organization.

I sometimes find myself humming Willie's country-and-western ballad during sessions when employees are playing "if only" in regard to their top management. As in, "If only he would take action and deal with all these complex and painful problems, we would be able to get on with business." Or, "If only we had her as our leader, she would get things squared away quickly and get us moving again!"

I first started humming this tune while attending an exclusive, invitation-only leadership conference, a gathering of prestigious academics and practitioners. I was struck by the ease with which even this savvy group accepted the great-savior theory of leadership. Our leaders have always been cowboys, and still are, it seems.

We tend to put our leaders on pedestals, to make them bigger than life. This deification plays out on both the positive and negative side at the national level. We believe that deeply rooted cultural and social problems can be solved if only we pick the right president. If he (or someday she) does well, we praise him; if not, we blame him, and woe betide him if he proves to have the kind of personal problems that we accept—even defend—in us lesser humans.

We also do this to leaders of other groups. We think that by getting Saddam Hussein we will be able to solve the social-economic-ethnic-theological tangle of the Middle East. Want to resolve political corruption in Central America? No problem! Just capture the current dictator (for example, Noriega). The way to fix the cocaine problem is to get rid of people like Pablo Escobar. There is no question that these bad guys deserved their fates, that isn't the point.

Deep down, we know that we can't cure underlying problems simply by shuffling leaders. Our own quality programs teach us that problems are rooted in processes and systems. Why, then, do we persist in worshipping our leaders when they succeed and beating on them when they fail?

We like our heroes and villains strong, simple, and clearly differentiated. We distrust ambiguity, equivocation, systems, and complexity. We want a *person* to praise or blame. Problems can be fixed, and that's why we have leaders. They represent us, and if they can't do the job we will get someone else. If we work in an overwhelmed organization and things seem hopeless, it is easier to blame the situation on top leadership than take action to deal with our survivor symptoms and take personal responsibility for learning.

Delegating our problems upward to a leader and waiting for success or failure to follow has not served our organizations well; too many are in trouble. Said differently, why is it that when we listen for Willie's soothing cowboy ballad, all we hear is something like the Rolling Stones belting out "I Can't Get No Satisfaction"? There are two reasons we often hear the wrong music.

The first is that we often forget that, in addition to its being a formal role vested in a person, leadership is also a process. Drath and Palus (1993) conceptualize leadership as a collective process in which we generate, maintain, and evolve meaning. In Herb Shepard's classic article, *Rules of Thumb for Change Agents* (1985), his Rule No. 6 calls for lighting many small fires. New-reality leadership is not a spectator sport. We all need to help each other move toward the learning response. We can all exercise *leadership* even though we don't all have formal roles as *leaders*.

The second reason we get no satisfaction is that we render our top leaders ineffective by deifying them. To the extent that we attribute godlike qualities to them, we dehumanize them, push them away, and cause them to be unable to develop or communicate empathy with the real pain felt by many of their fellow survivors.

As a consequence, many of our top leaders are figureheads and actors. This is not all their fault, nor is it all ours. As they say, it takes two to tango. On one side, it's difficult to resist being treated like a god. On the other side, we scripted the roles they are acting out. There are a lot of other forces, including general cultural expectations, that cause our formal leaders to persist in this destructive relationship. We can, however, do our part by reducing our expectations and taking personal responsibility. Although the following suggestions are intended for top managers, they will also be of assistance to those of us who want to break the pattern of collusion and help our leaders to be more effective.

Don't Let Them Make You into a Savior

You are not Clint Eastwood and will not be able to get all the bad guys without lots of help. Find ways to show your humanity. If you don't have an answer, say so. If you are confused, let others know. If you are sad and emotional because your friends and colleagues are being laid off, act that way. To the extent you exhibit your human vulnerability, you will enable others to take responsibility and display leadership behaviors that could just save your organization.

Manage By "Being" Around, Not "Walking" Around

An entire generation of managers has grown up perpetuating the myth of the charismatic leader *walking around*, acting confident and being a cheerleader to *them*, those others. It's as if *they* can't walk around; as if walking around is something the top does to the middle and bottom. This is a cowboy attitude. First, it sets up the false dynamics of those who are up (the walkers) and those who are down (the visited). Of course, like Clint when he walks around assuring the townfolks that he, and he alone, will clean out the bad guys, it sets up a dependency relationship. Second, I know of no evidence that charisma, which is what is usually being dispensed in the walks, has much to do with real leadership; in fact, I think it often gets in the way.

Visiting with no charisma is also a problem. I have seen highly introverted and analytical leaders go out and attempt to fake it after reading a book or listening to the coaching of their human resource vice presidents. Often they come off as badly cast actors in a very artificial role. *Being around* means behaving authentically, being who you are and acting in accord with your true nature. Mingling with other parts of the organization is a good idea, but walking around with a script written by lawyers or professional communicators comes off as contrived.

Another part of being around involves getting rid of false and therefore distance-inducing status symbols. It is difficult to convince others in the organization that you are really interested in empowering them and being part of their world when you wall them off with separate dining areas, reserved parking spaces, and secluded and often elaborately guarded office suites.

Seek Feedback

Being a cowboy is seductive. I'm sure the boot hills of the Old West are filled with gunfighters who believed in their own invulnerability. Top leaders need to work very hard to find objective information about themselves. Even in the best organizations, people are going to pull their punches when dealing with the top echelon. Feedback from multiple sources—from peers and subordinates as well as from bosses—can be a powerful tool. Leaders attempting to share leadership, be congruent, and empower others need to find ways to get valid data on themselves.

Tend to Your Own Learning

Top managers are employees too. You need to assess your own R-type and take the steps necessary to learn how to learn. This isn't an easy process. For sure, cowboy leaders—colluding with those who would grant them omniscient, godlike qualities—do not easily open themselves to new learnings.

The creation of a learning culture requires a dual application of courage. Formal leaders need the bravery to stop playing cowboy and to express their human vulnerability, and the rest of us need the fortitude to exercise leadership and not delegate upward. If we get our act together, we just might be able to stop singing cowboy ballads and all join in a rousing rendition of "We Shall Overcome"—with an emphasis on the "we"!

The New Leadership Imperative

Leadership in the new reality involves letting go of past assumptions about what leaders do, how they are trained and developed, and how they relate to the rest of the organization. As we have seen, to be relevant, top managers need to get off their horses, hang up their spurs, roll up their sleeves, and establish an authentic relationship with their fellow employees. The rest of the organization needs to enable them to do this by allowing them to be human.

Bringing old-paradigm assumptions as to what constitutes useful leadership into the new reality often creates frustration, which can generate cynicism in some leaders. Reacting to the future with a cynical victimhood is not a way to lead either a life or an organization. It is, therefore, essential to check the validity of our assumptions as to what new-paradigm leaders actually do.

What Leaders Do: Paul's Prescription

I met Paul in a building often described by managers in his East-coast high-tech organization as "The Elephants' Burial Ground." This referenced the practice of aging elephants, knowing their time was past, slipping away from the herd and going to a remote section of the wilderness to die. Paul's corporate burial ground was a small facility, a few miles from the organization's headquarters, where out-placed executives moved until they found another job or their contract expired. The contract was a consulting agreement whereby the displaced executives would *help* the organization. In reality, it was a way of keeping them on the payroll while they made the transition out. The offices were plush, complete with the requisite executive desk, credenza, and bookshelf; in strict compliance with the authorized perquisites to which their rank entitled them as outlined in the company policy manual. They even had individual executive secretaries who sat outside their offices ready to answer their phones on those rare occasions when they rang. Paul and his fellow "executives in transition" had everything except something organizationally relevant to do.

Most of Paul's fellow graveyard denizens were doing external things: networking and looking for jobs, managing their investments, or simply using their offices as places to get away from home and plan lunches and golf matches with their friends. Paul did none of these things. He not only refused to work with the organization's outplacement firm, but he really believed the organization wanted him to be a consultant and persisted in looking for something to do. This had two bad effects: it kept him from moving away from a past that needed to be dropped, and it annoyed and distracted his potential clients back in the organization, most of whom were a couple of levels below him in the hierarchy and felt the need to be nice to him. My task: "Try and talk some sense into Paul!"

The first thing I noticed as I entered his office was a framed cartoon on the wall behind his desk. It had a picture of a very mean-looking vulture who was speaking to a friend. The caption said, "Patience Hell. Let's Go Out and Kill Something." Paul had a lot of signs in his office. One near the door reminded visitors that, "It's not creative unless it sells." I agreed! What I was attempting to do was creatively sell Paul the fact that nothing good would happen to him unless he let go of the past. In his case, that past centered on a truculent belief that the way leaders functioned in times of trauma and transition was, in his words, to "tough it out" while "maintaining positive communications in all directions." In my words, Paul thought he could sell his way out of any problem. The selling was tridimensional. The first sale was to himself; there was no problem that hard work and bluster could not overcome and he had plenty of slogans to support this, of "the tough get going when the going gets tough" genre. The second sale was to his fellow employees and took the form of the "quit bitching and get to work" mantra. The third sale involved external customers. It didn't matter if his organization's products were obsolete and the customers didn't want to see him. He had plenty of slogans of the "if you knock on enough doors, one will open" variety.

Paul was an honest, sincere executive. Despite his current response pattern, which placed him in the uninformed optimist section of the BS box, he was once—in the distant past of the old paradigm—an effective manager. There is nothing wrong with motivational slogans, trite or otherwise, and certainly focus on the customer is a primary path out of the doldrums of layoff survivor sickness. Paul's problem was that he was using slogans and uninformed optimism to reinforce a past that was no longer organizationally functional or personally relevant. He was blocking his learning by hiding behind his stilted sales rhetoric. In classic BS style, Paul was conning himself. Paul's prescription as to what new-paradigm leaders do was wrong. In fact, pharmacologically speaking, it was contraindicated. Leaders do not try to tough it out and sell their way into the new reality.

What Leaders Do: Silicon Soldiers from MBA Land

I recently spent a few days at a quantitatively oriented business school, one that equips students to do complex analytical problem solving. The students were brilliant, with off-the-scale SAT scores and the analytical ability and computer skills to reduce any issue to a mathematical model that could be dealt with in a dispassionate and rational manner. Most of the young and equally brilliant faculty were in hot-blooded, lusty pursuit of the holy grail of tenure. In this university, the tenure trail took them into the abstract land of theoretical models, quantitative analysis, and publication in narrow refereed journals. The older faculty, more staid and traditional if less brilliant, were focused on narrow lines of academic pursuit in collaboration with a small number of equally constricted academic colleagues from other institutions. Needless to say, there was a gap between the so-called real world as I experienced it in organizations and that envisioned by many of the students and faculty members of that business school.

A problem encountered by some graduates of this institution when they joined the dynamic and imperfect world of commerce was articulated by a recent graduate who was back on campus on a recruiting trip and joined me for lunch. He recounted his first weeks with his employer, an international financial services firm. I had my tape recorder with me and what follows is an edited, paraphrased version of what he had to say.

"The first day was great. They had an orientation with some other MBAs, went over the benefits and the history of the firm. The second day, they sent me to find my new boss, only there was a reorganization in process and no one seemed to know why I was there or even what department to put me in. By the third day, they found out I knew how to do spreadsheets and I ended up in front of a terminal analyzing small business loans. I did that for a few days but no one really cared because they had decided to move small business lending to another division. I kind of floated around for a couple of months, then there was a really big layoff and lots of more senior people hit the street. They didn't touch me—I guess because I was too new and they didn't want to ruin their reputation with the school—laying off a new MBA grad.

"I have now been with them three years. I've kind of found a home with a small group in the marketing department. I really like the place, but it is absolutely different from what I expected going in. We reorganize every few months, there are always layoffs going on somewhere, there is constant confusion and no one really knows who does what. We make decisions without any lead time, walking down the hall, in random meetings, by hunch and gut feel. I don't even have time to set up those decision models I learned here! My message to this school is to get real. They really don't have a clue what happens out there—they need to teach us how to manage in a world of confusion and stress. They could benefit by going out and working for a while to get a feel for what it is really like these days."

The message brought back by this recent graduate, fresh from his initial baptism of fire, was the myth of rationality. Organizations of the new reality are not orderly, rational places where logic, analysis, and cool contemplation are the underpinnings of management action. They are chaotic, confusing, and filled with conflicting values, choices, and demands. Just as Newton's vision of a fixed, predictable, clockwork universe has been undone by the theory of relativity, so has the notion of a rational, calm organization been replaced by a much more messy, creative, and unpredictable reality. Managing in such an organization requires very different skills and perspectives from those of the past. Calmly rational analysis and logical and deliberate decision making are not what leaders of the new reality do. These techniques are as far off the mark as Paul's uninformed blustering and truculent optimism.

What Leaders Really Do: Facilitation of Transitions

Neither Paul's idea of new-reality leaders as macho sloganeers who sell yesterday's solutions to tomorrow's problems nor the business-school notion of managers as calm quantitative analyzers is correct. What organizational leaders who really make a difference do is to facilitate transitions. They know they can't stay relevant to the needs of new-reality organizations by doggedly holding on to the theories and practices of the past. They don't try to help their organizations survive by applying a Newtonian theory of predictable rationality, or by shooting all the snakes (that is, dealing with symptoms and not root causes, as discussed in Chapter One).

What will make the difference between those organizations that make it in the new reality and those that will not is the cultivation of leaders with the ability to facilitate transitions: their own, the organization's, and those of their fellow employees. Table 8.1 describes three types of transition facilitation competencies for new-reality leaders.

• *Self-transition.* Contrary to the orientation of many academic studies and reports from the popular media, there is no major

Table 8.1. Three Levels of Transition Facilitation.

SCOPE	COMPETENCY	SKILLS
Self	Intrapersonal insight	• Self-awareness • Clarity of own needs and agenda • Valid data on how perceived by others
Work Group	Interpersonal competence	• Empathetic listening • Ability to give and receive feedback • Ability to reflect feelings and emotions • Coaching and counseling ability • An operating model and a theory of transition
Total Organization	Ability to stimulate collective dialogue	• Courage and discipline to refrain from individual action taking • Belief (faith) that collective learning and problem solving provides better answers

division between *managers* and *them*. Managers are portrayed as doing things to "them"—that is, to the great mass of employees. Managers, supervisors, directors, vice presidents, and even presidents are employees too, and have things done to them as well as doing things to others. In the new-reality organization, arbitrary distinctions between managers and the masses are misleading, and perpetuate inaccurate stereotypes.

To be relevant to the true needs of organizations, leaders need to begin with their own transitions. This is often a very difficult process for those who came up under one set of assumptions and norms and now must let go of some of the basic skills that got them to the top before they can help the organization survive. Some, like Paul, find the pain too great, and take the path of denial by stubbornly holding on to the past and refusing to open up to new options. This results in the entrenched or the BS response pattern. For those with the courage to try, it is a voyage of discovery. The old adage is really true: you can't help others unless you help yourself. The basic competency is intrapersonal insight and the primary tool for this self-understanding is valid feedback.

• *Work group transition.* Take out a clean piece of lined paper. List on one line those who are immediately above you in the organization: your boss and others on that level with whom you regularly interact. Next, drop a few lines and list those who work for you and others at that level with whom you interact. Finally, in the space between, list those peers with whom you have the most interaction. Put yourself in the middle and draw a circle. You now have a 360-degree sphere of influence, what I call your work group. The picture may look calm and in control to you, but if your organization is like most, you can bet that all these people are struggling with their own uncertainties, fears, and confusion. They are behaving according to their individual R-types. You can help each of them move toward the learning response—or if they are already there, to hold onto it. To the extent you can help each of them better let go of the past, refocus their self-esteem from where they work to what they do, and move their attention from internal politics and relationships to helping serve customers, you are exercising the type of leadership that will increase your organization's survival. It will help you, them, and your organization break free. The core competency is what Chris Argyris (1970) called "interpersonal competence." The tools of interpersonal competence are basic helping skills: empathetic listening, giving and receiving feedback in a nondefensive manner, reflecting feelings and emotions, and coaching and counseling. Effective leaders working at this level also require a clear theory in regard to the transition and change process.

- *Total organization transition.* You don't have to be the CEO to help move the organization into the upper right quadrant of the R-factor model. As Herb Shepard wrote (1985, p. 4), "If many interdependent subsystems are catalyzed, and the change agent brings them together to facilitate one another's efforts, the entire system can begin to move."

Organizations of the future will not survive without becoming communities of learning. The learning organization is no academic fad or consultant's buzz word. It is absolutely essential for organizations to learn from their environments, to continually adjust to new and changing data, and, just as is the case with the individual, to learn how to learn from an uncertain and unpredictable future. Leadership competencies include the ability to stimulate and engage in a true collective dialogue. This requires the courage and discipline to go against the grain of cowboy fix-it-and-ride-out-of-town expectations. Leaders must have the patience to refrain from taking individual action until the community reformats and redirects the issues. It also requires faith that collective problem solving and learning will, in the long term, be better than the traditional cowboy style. Leadership at this level is captured in three very powerful words: courage, discipline, and faith!

Action-Oriented Facilitation Activities

What follows are ten very specific and prescriptive activities that will facilitate the development of basic transition facilitation skills.

These activities cut across all three levels shown in Table 8.1, and are presented at random. There is no meaning to position on the list.

- *Attend a good, old fashioned T-group.* Yes, this is sensitivity training, and yes, it is "feely"—but it probably won't be "touchy." The bottom line is that this kind of laboratory training is a very powerful way to get the depth of feedback that will lead to self-awareness. It is important to assure yourself that the facilitators are professional and the organization sponsoring the session has a track record with organizational managers.

- *Complete a professional 360-degree feedback instrument.* By professional, I mean that you should use an instrument that has a history, validity standards, and norms. Have the results interpreted by someone trained in helping you understand what it means and doesn't mean. Some organizations have their own 360-degree instruments and others use instruments licensed and certified by external vendors. There are also some excellent external organizations you can hire to administer such instruments.

- *Attend a professional leadership training program.* This type of training is different from a program on marketing, Total Quality Management, or performance management. By professional, I mean that it should be either put on by a reliable external organization focusing on leadership training or by a similarly oriented and competent internal group. In either case, the focus should be on the skills outlined in Table 8.1. There are some very good in-house programs and some excellent external offerings.

- *Take evening courses or sign up for special programs that teach helping skills.* The bad news, at least for the validity of their curricula, is that these kinds of offerings are not often found in business schools. The good news is that they can be found in other schools and departments such as psychology, sociology, counseling, organization development, and educational psychology. There are also one-time seminars and special programs put on by universities and consulting organizations.

- *Become familiar with future search technology.* There is a whole new movement out there, using labels such as "future search" and

speaking of "getting the whole system in a room." These large sys-
tems-change processes go for the jugular in stimulating collective
learning! If you want to jump-start your understanding of learning
in the collective, you need to get on the bandwagon; the technology is growing faster than it can be codified. There are an increasing number of seminars and workshops and some excellent books
and articles (for example, see Weisbord, 1992; Bunker and Alban,
1992, 1997; Emery and Purser, 1996).

• *Learn how to have a dialogue.* A dialogue is different from a
discussion, an argument, a debate, or a business meeting. The dialogue process is very important in developing learning organizations
and is central to collective learning. There are seminars and workshops. You can also find some consultants who can teach you and
your organization dialogue skills.

• *Find a truth teller.* It is particularly important for top managers to cultivate and use truth tellers. A truth teller is someone in
the organization you can rely on to "call them the way they see
them," and give you straight, unfiltered feedback. The best truth
tellers have three characteristics: they are tuned in to what is going
on at all levels of the organization—top, middle, and bottom; they
are secure and have no personal ax to grind; and you trust them.

• *Get involved in the leadership of a volunteer organization.* Pick
one that does not receive funding or support from your organization. Helping manage a volunteer organization is a powerful feedback and developmental experience. It removes you from your
positional power base and allows you to assess your true impact. It's
very different when people don't have to listen to you or tell you
what you want to hear. Many volunteer organizations are fraction-
ated, political, and made up of conflicting special interest groups.
Yet they have to accomplish something. What better way to learn
how to merge single interests into the collective good?

• *Get active in your professional association.* Don't just attend
the national meeting—become a worker, serve on committees, pass
out the literature, do time in the information booth, set up the

chairs. The higher you are, the more the value of the grunt work. It forces you to see an organizational system from a different perspective and helps you rethink your own skills and assumptions as to what constitutes value-added.

•   *Set up an intensive personal feedback project.* One option involves retaining an external consultant to nearly overwhelm you with feedback, armed with a wide range of data points and assessment instruments. This is a very intensive and impressive process. You can't escape the data, and a skilled consultant will help you understand it and do something with it. A second approach involves using an internal consultant, probably someone from the organizational development, training, or human resources function. I have seen internal consultants do excellent work—but none of us are prophets in our own land. Depending on your level and your organization's culture, an external consultant may be better regardless of the competence of the internal person.

The Complexity of Meeting People Where They Are

A basic consultant's guideline is to meet clients where they are, not where you want them to be. This doesn't mean the location of lunch, or whether a January retreat should be scheduled in Minnesota or Florida. It is a meeting in psychological space, not physical space, and it is a hard meeting to arrange. Despite our sincere desire to be objective and nonjudgmental, we all—consultants and organizational leaders alike—see things through our own lenses, our own values, and our own sense of how things ought to or should be. New-paradigm leadership, like competent consulting, is complex and fraught with value conflicts. A basic component of intrapersonal insight is to be clear and own our oughts and shoulds, while accepting data that says what is. For organizational leaders, this not only means meeting employees where they are, it also means accepting that being there is their reality. Connecting with people in their own psychological space in a manner that minimizes getting hooked by our own shoulds and oughts is important for all levels of the organization. As an example of how frequently we meet others where we think they ought to be as opposed to where they are, I have paraphrased three two-sentence interactions that will be familiar to many who reside in organizations:

Interaction One

CONSULTANT: The survey and follow-on interviews show conclusively that your middle management population is angry, anxious, confused, and looking for direction.

CEO: They *shouldn't* feel that way; they *ought* to feel good about our progress.

Interaction Two

HUMAN RESOURCES VICE PRESIDENT: I spent the morning with the financial planning people and they still think the payroll is too big. We need to have more reductions.

TRAINING DIRECTOR: "They *should* have more concern for people and, if they think it's so easy, they *ought* to do the dirty work themselves.

Interaction Three

FIRST LINE SUPERVISOR: Our headcount budget got cut and we're not going to be able to hire two of the people you requested.

PROJECT ENGINEER: He *should* get out of the ivory tower and they *ought* to understand that we need this project staffed properly.

These *should* and *ought* interactions illustrate four important points for leaders attempting to meet people where they are and facilitate transitions:

- *Organizations experience transitions differentially by level.* Bridges (1980) outlines a three-step process for going through transitions: an ending, a neutral zone, and a new beginning. He emphasizes that we can't move directly from an ending to a new beginning; we need to spend insightful and regenerative time in the neutral zone. This is an uncertain time, when we are neither in the old or in the new. Using this model, what I often see in organizations is that the top has gone through the neutral zone, had an ending, and is well into a new beginning, while the middle is still wallowing in the neutral zone, and the bottom hasn't yet begun the process. Organizations tend to go through their endings, neutral zones, and beginnings hierarchically.

• *Organizations experience transitions differentially by "silo."* Certain functions tend to go through transitions faster than others. In many organizations the financial and sales functions seem to move from endings through the neutral zone and into new beginnings at a more rapid rate than others such as human resources or manufacturing.

• *Organizations experience transitions differentially by R-type.* In large, decentralized organizations, there are often subcultures of R-types. Those divisions or subunits that are closer to the learning response will move from ending to new beginning much more rapidly than overwhelmed units, who remain in the neutral zone much longer.

• *Organizations experience multiple waves of transitions.* In an environment of unending change, organizations are always in the process of traveling the path of endings, neutral zones, and beginnings. What makes the situation even more complex is that different levels, functions, and R-types are on different paths. In most organizations, there are many transitions going on simultaneously and they are not the same transition. For example, the top could have gone through the transition from a job-security environment to a temp-employment environment, then moved on to another transition—say from centralization to decentralization—and be working on a third transition such as moving from a product-driven to a market-driven strategy. Those two levels below the top could still be working on the decentralization transition, and lower middle management could still be struggling with the initial job-security transition. When differences by function and by R-type are factored in, the complexity of the transition process becomes apparent.

Advice for Leaders

I have three final thoughts for leaders who are attempting to understand where people are and meet them in their psychological space:

- *Mistrust your assumptions—seek data.* With the confusion of different levels, functions, and cultures going through different transitions at different speeds, it is difficult to figure out where people are, let alone meet them there. It is very complex, and unchecked assumptions without data do not open the path to understanding.

- *Don't send—receive.* When you mention communications to many top managers, they think in terms of sending messages, and they do a lot of it as is evidenced by the volume of newsletters, memos, speeches, and videos working their way down the hierarchy. Top managers send far too often and receive far too seldom. It is a two-pronged problem. First, top managers get hooked because employees keep asking for communication when what they are really seeking is hope and assurance. There are more meaningful ways of providing hope and assurance than top-down formal communications. Second, top management controls the internal communications media and easily fall prey to the delusion that such media offer the best way to get all their own oughts and shoulds off their chests and out of their hearts.

If you are a top manager, you need to resist the temptation to use your internal communications machinery to grind your own ax. When parts of the organization are two or three transitions behind you, they are not interested in your current vision or where you are on your current transition effort. What is really important to your role as chief transition facilitator is to receive information, to listen, and to discover where other people are in their transitions. If you don't do that and only send, you are not only flying blind, you are preaching to the deaf.

- *Cultivate multiple data points—and respect their message.* To receive valid information, leaders need to offset the hierarchical communications filters that exist in all organizations. The best way to get around the universal institutional impulse to manage and control the news is to establish nontraditional communication links throughout the organization. The objective is to set up multiple data points. The next step involves remaining open to hearing all the shoulds and oughts even though they are not yours, and you may not agree with them.

Five Fallacies

Transition facilitation is the currency of the realm for those who hope to lead new-reality organizations. Unfortunately, many leaders are undercapitalized. While it may be true that these aren't the skills that got them where they are, it is also true that without them they won't be able to stay there very long.

I once spent a few hours with a select group of so-called high-potential employees. It was not my intended topic, but because of what was going on in their organization and their keen interest, we spent most of our time working on helping skills and discussing transition theory. It was a great session and everyone felt good about it. Everyone, that is, with the exception of the CEO who was next on the agenda and had spent five minutes waiting for me to finish. He opened his speech by telling the group he was going to stick to his subject and talk about real business issues as opposed to the "soft" and presumably (to him) irrelevant "stuff" they had just heard. Unfortunately, too many top executives feel that way. In these days of short-term planning, with executive compensation pegged to fixing symptoms and not root causes (institutionalized snake shooting), too many boards of directors and too many search committees share that ex-CEO's opinion. (Yes, he is no longer there and not by choice. There is some justice!)

Today there are a large number of organizations in trouble because of their entrenched and overwhelmed cultures. Yet we persist in promoting and hiring leaders who not only lack the requisite knowledge but actively devalue the very skills and perspectives that can save their organizations. Part of the reason is that many top executives, boards, and search committees are operating from false premises. What follows are five of these frequently occurring fallacies and corresponding realities:

• *Fallacy One*. Self-understanding is soft. Real leaders deal with the hard stuff—like making the bottom line or making a payroll. They don't have time for navel gazing.

Reality One. The courage to seek feedback, to face the reality that the script that you wrote and think you are acting out is not only misunderstood by others but is often inappropriate to the needs of the organization, is not soft at all. We must find the fortitude to look in the mirror, and that is perhaps the hardest thing any of us can do!

• *Fallacy Two*. Marketing, finance, new product development—those are the activities that turn organizations around. The soft side is something real line managers don't have time for. That's why organizations have consultants, HR people, and psychologists.

Reality Two. Transition facilitation is the essence of line management in the new reality! Functional excellence is important, but by itself will not keep your organization afloat. The primary leadership task involves harnessing human spirit to help customers. In a time of paradigm change, this involves facilitating transition. This cannot be delegated, abstracted, or consigned to the doldrums of a task force. It requires active personal involvement by line management.

• *Fallacy Three*. Real managers don't have the time, energy, or skills to go around playing shrink or confessor to others. They have problems themselves.

Reality Three. If not you, who? You are smart, that's how you got where you are. You can learn how to help others cope with the stress of transition. That's what they are really paying you to do. It is the best use of your time if you and your organization are serious about surviving.

• *Fallacy Four*. If top management found out people were spending time facilitating transitions and doing all the rest of that soft stuff, heads would roll. They want to cut costs and increase productivity—to do more with less.

Reality Four. What your management really wants you to do is to help keep your organization afloat, to focus on customers, to help and delight them. You can't do that without a liberated, non-codependent work force and you don't get there or stay there without that so-called soft stuff. P.S. It is really hard stuff!

- *Fallacy Five.* Now that the economy has turned around and the organization has money again, all this stuff about transition and change is in the past. What we need now is to return to basics—keep doing what made us great in the first place.

Reality Five. Like it or not, things have changed and they have changed irrevocably. Even with a return to profitability the fundamental relationship of person to job has changed. There is no longer a lifetime contract, and helping understand and facilitate the basic transition into that new reality is the essence of leadership.

Liberation Leadership: Perspective and Observations

Leadership in the new reality is neither a gentle nor a spectator sport. It is an against-the-grain activity requiring tenacity, courage, and faith. Seeking the difficult and elusive systemic solution, while resisting the shallow and often-reinforced short-term fix, requires tenacity. Learning and behaving according to the relevant but new soft competencies, while resisting the temptation to retreat into the easier and irrelevant hard behaviors of the past, requires courage. Resisting the pressure for individual action, while allowing collective learning to take place, requires faith.

Leadership is more than a person occupying a role, it is a process that can be shared. In all its manifestations, liberation leadership is exceptionally important. It has the potential to free individuals and organizations. It can facilitate the learning that will help individuals break their codependence and allow them to apply their human spirit to their work. It can help build organizations that will thrive and grow through collective learning.

Angling Lessons

The old, often-cited Chinese proverb, "Give a man a fish and you feed him for a day. Teach a man to fish and you feed him for a lifetime" (Tripp, 1970), captures the essential challenge of developing employees with the ability to function in a complex and uncertain future. Learning how to fish is the core developmental challenge of the new reality. It is sophomoric to assume that we can really predict what competencies will be relevant to an environment of unending change. Although many of the skills of the past will no doubt continue to be necessary, the essential ingredient needed to assure organizational survival will be a workforce of skilled anglers.

Janet's Fishing School

The cluttered classroom overlooked a parking lot. It was not an inspiring view at the best of times and late in a cold, dark, December afternoon, the only thing the street lamp illuminated was a dumpster, half buried by a pile of dirty snow. It was an unusual place to learn how to fish but, then, Janet was an unusual instructor.

I was guided through a labyrinth of twists, turns, long corridors, and stairways. After a long walk, I was ushered into the classroom. It was located deep in the bowels of the corporate headquarters of an upper-Midwest high-technology organization. Janet was a member of the training staff and was just completing a session of a course with the title "Creative Problem Solving Techniques." It was a required course in the organization's middle-management core curriculum.

The middle-management workforce in Janet's organization was populated by a large number of employees with R-entrenched behavior patterns—and most of them were not excited about attending any training, let alone courses mandated by what they called "corporate." The corporate staff–directed core curriculum was not working, and Janet's creative problem solving course was the only offering that received good evaluations and was consistently overbooked. Clearly Janet was doing something right and the purpose of my visit that dark December afternoon was to discover what that was.

When I entered the classroom, she was completing a module on statistical process control, a requirement dictated by the staff of her organization's Total Quality Management program. Most of the participants in that particular course were from field-based organizations, with a large representation from the marketing division. I was amazed at their spirit and attitude. Control charts and histograms are not topics that make the earth move for most sales and marketing types.

"I'm not just teaching a module in the company's management core curriculum," she said with a twinkle in her eye and a tone of exaggerated seriousness. Janet—no stranger to the Chinese proverb—continued, "I'm giving them fishing lessons."

She continued with the metaphor, pointing out that it was cold in her location in December, and the only way to do any fishing was by walking or driving out on the ice and cutting a hole, a matter requiring some skill for those not interested in impromptu swimming. However, in the spring the trout streams were open and fly fishing called for a different set of skills, which were in turn very different from the ones required for lake fishing in the heat of August.

"Who knows what kind of fishing will be appropriate in the future?" she asked. "Trolling in the ocean, casting in the river, netting the shallows, spears? And what kind of fish will there be and what kind of bait will work?"

She explained that she couldn't officially own up to her real teaching goal. It was too complex and paradoxical to be politically correct in her organization's entrenched culture. It was the stuff of the new reality. On one level, she was attempting to help her students develop the analytical skills necessary to scan and make sense out of a changing and unpredictable business environment. At another level, she was teaching them the futility of holding on to any narrow techniques, including the ones she was teaching them.

"I'm helping them to 'know when to hold 'em, and know when to fold 'em,'" she said. "We will all have to have the ability to develop our own techniques to fit the times. We have to learn how to fish!"

Although she didn't articulate it, Janet was in the business of teaching her students how to learn how to learn. She was a gifted teacher and used three techniques central to facilitating the learning response:

• *Pushing learning in unnatural directions*. Learning to learn is not a natural act. It is an against-the-grain experience. In teaching people how to fish, she was, in essence, teaching them how to access different learning tactics and use unfamiliar skills. She not only taught statistical process control techniques to salespeople, she also taught empathy skills to engineers.

• *Being intentional and analytical about the learning process*. She made her students keep learning journals. They had to write down what they learned, how they learned it, and most important, what they learned about the process of learning. The process of journaling for many of them was itself an against-the-grain experience, and she made them write about that too.

• *Organizing support groups*. Small-group work was an integral part of Janet's fishing school. The class was broken down into what she called learning groups, which functioned as primary reference groups for feedback, coaching, and goal setting. Going against the grain is a stressful process for even the best learners and human support systems are essential.

Edgar's Epistemological Embarrassment

Edgar was a young doctoral student in the applied behavioral sciences who—unlike many of his colleagues—focused a substantial portion of his graduate education on the history of science and philosophy, and thus both amused and enlightened his colleagues that summer by regularly using words like "ontology" and "epistemology." As a part of a summer internship, he accompanied me to a meeting with a very practical—some would even say crusty—hands-on human resources director. Our data showed that the workforce in his organization was angry, internally oriented, and gridlocked by analysis paralysis. They needed to be enticed out of the refuge of the entrenched and focused on helping customers. It was the purpose of our visit to share this information and engage in a discussion of options for doing something about it. I thought it would be good experience for Edgar to deliver the initial feedback. What followed were two classic lines of dialogue that never failed to crack up our staff and clients when the anecdote got told and retold that summer, and still do, when repeated on the proper occasion.

Edgar's opening was to look the director in the eye and say with great sincerity, "They are epistemologically undernourished!"

After a long, theatrically thoughtful pause, our client responded in his best Southern drawl, "E-pissed-uh what?" Then with a smile, "Someone hungry?"

"What he means is that they need to get closer to the customer," I interjected, losing the battle to hold back my laughter.

I don't know if our street-smart client knew the definition of epistemology or not but I suspect he did. I do know he gave Edgar a valuable lesson, which was his intent. That lesson was to communicate with clients in their language about their needs, not to satisfy the consultant's need to impress the client. Sincere asides about people or organizations being "epistemologically undernourished," followed by "E-pissed-uh what?" delivered in deep-voiced drawls, became a standard day-brightener that summer. Although the timing and context of Edgar's pronouncement was not appropriate, the concept of epistemological malnutrition is very powerful when thinking about underutilized learning tactics, and stimulates the following general observations:

• *Learning to learn is an epistemological process.* It deals with the origin and limits of knowledge. To move the entrenched toward more relevant behavior, stop the negative slide of the overwhelmed, or break up the BSers' narcissistic ignorance, it is necessary to illuminate blind spots and reveal what we don't know or what we believe is not relevant to know. The process involves stimulating the use of underutilized learning tactics. Edgar was right on; most people are epistemologically undernourished, that is, they need new frames of reference and access to undiscovered options.

• *New learning tactics lead to new insights.* Insight provides the means to epistemological nutrition and insight is stimulated by new learning tactics. Edgar emerged from that summer with the understanding that his need to impress others got in the way of his need to help others. He came to that insight not through his primary past learning tactic of thinking, but through a different process: accessing others. Thus, he had a double learning, a deeper insight into the impact of his agenda on others, and the realization that he could not have achieved that insight without new learning tactics.

• *We need to meet others where they are, not where we want them to be.* Most people are epistemologically undernourished, they are locked into narrow learning tactics. Just as the human resources director reminded Edgar that he wanted to see the issues in his context and through his lenses, those of us attempting to help employees develop new and more relevant learning tactics need to begin with their epistemological orientation, not ours. If we don't want to further embed the entrenched or hasten the descent of the overwhelmed, we need to go slowly, use their context, and nudge them into more relevant learning options.

- *No matter how they got here or where they are going, they are here now.* Edgar and the human resources director met in the here and now, up close and personal. Although they came to that office through very different paths, and would, no doubt, go very different directions in the future, they were together at that point in time, and the phenomenological reality was that they had to deal with each other. There are many compelling and powerful theories concerning human growth, development, and learning (for example, see Maslow, 1954; Rogers, 1961; Kegan, 1982). It is a broad and diverse stream of research and theory. However, like Edgar, we meet our organizational colleagues in the here and now, within a unique phenomenological horizon. Our staffing programs do not screen for developmental stages and our career planning models do not account for differing frames of self- and organizational differentiation. In the new reality, we need to help people develop better learning tactics where we find them, regardless of what stage they may be in any developmental sequence. The learning tactics model illustrated in Figure 9.1 is designed to help employees assess and plan more balanced and intentional learning tactics in the here and now, and it works within the context of longer-term developmental theories.

The Learning Tactics Model

The four dimensions of the learning tactics model (LTM) were developed during a year-long exploratory study working with high-potential managers (Bunker and Webb, 1992). The roots of this study can, in turn, be traced to the development of the R-factor model (see Appendix B). The Learning Tactics Model is a descriptive and exploratory model designed to serve as an integrating frame of reference and help people in organizations understand and make

Figure 9.1. Learning Tactics Model.

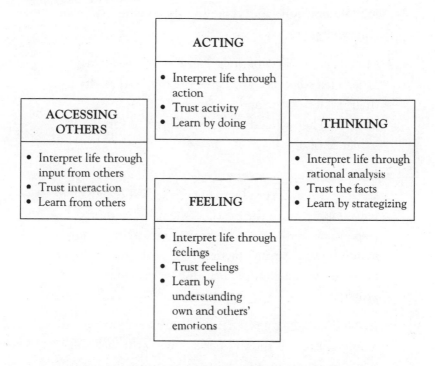

choices concerning the relevance of their learning tactics. What follows are ten observations and tentative conclusions concerning the model and how it relates to organizational managers and leaders:

Using the Learning Tactics Model

- *Most managers have a single preferred learning style.* They are overdependent on one tactic (one box in the Learning Tactics Model), and fail to consider other options. They are not intentional in matching their learning tactics to the problem they are dealing with.

- *This preferred style has remained constant over time and event.* This primary learning tactic has been reinforced by past assignments, early childhood experience, and parental commandments. Its use can be traced through high school, college, and family and community problem solving.

- *Most managers go through the four learning tactics in a preferential sequence.* They give the highest priority to their primary tactic and the lowest to their least favorite. They often do not consider the entire sequence of options.

- *It is important that managers be flexible and use a variety of learning tactics.* To productively engage issues and challenges and grow in the process (the basic learning response pattern), it is necessary to be intentional in matching the learning tactic to the problem. It is often necessary to use multiple learning tactics on the same problem.

- *It is difficult for most managers to break set.* Starting with a different box in the LTM and moving through the boxes in a different sequence is an against-the-grain experience. Matching the learning challenge to the learning tactic requires restraint and discipline.

- *Most managers can learn how to do it.* Managers are smart and much more adaptable and flexible than many—often including themselves—believe. Breaking set, going against the grain, and developing a wider repertoire of learning tactics can and has been learned by midcareer managers.

- *There is a short-term price for breaking set.* The cost of breaking set and pursuing new learning tactics is discomfort, a feeling of awkwardness, and often a short-term decline in performance.

- *There is a long-term payoff for breaking set.* The long-term payoff for developing a more flexible response to matching learning tactic to problem is immense. It will help assure individual relevance and organizational survival.

- *New learning tactics stimulate better response patterns.* Learning new and more appropriate learning tactics will move the entrenched employee out of the bunker, provide the insight necessary to break the BS pattern, and pull the overwhelmed employee out of a descent into irrelevance.

- *New learning tactics lead to better decisions.* In the working world of the adult manager, decision making, problem solving, and learning are impossible to separate. Adults learn when they need to learn and in organizations that need is almost always focused on a problem to be solved and a decision to be made. Intentional and multitactic learning will result in better problem solving and decisions that solve root causes and not symptoms.

Learning Options

Each of the four options in Figure 9.1 represents a way of interpreting reality (an operant paradigm), a methodological process for problem solving, and a primary learning tactic.

Taking Action

- *Operant paradigm.* The way to make sense out of life is to do something; take action; make something happen.

- *Problem-solving process.* Problems are solved by trial and error while engaged in the issue. Gut feeling and unarticulated intuition are the guides. Motto: "Just do it!"

- *Learning tactic.* Learn by doing.

Thinking

- *Operant paradigm*. Making sense involves logical analysis of information, which leads to knowledge.

- *Problem-solving process*. Problems are solved by assessing and analyzing the facts. This is an individual activity. Motto: "Think it through."

- *Learning tactic*. Learn by strategizing.

Feeling

- *Operant paradigm*. Making sense involves personal feelings and emotions.

- *Problem-solving process*. Problems are connected to interpersonal relationships. Motto: "How does it feel?"

- *Learning tactic*. Learn by understanding your own and others' emotions.

Accessing Others

- *Operant paradigm*. Making sense occurs through direct or indirect input from other people.

- *Problem-solving process*. Problems are solved by connecting with others. Motto: "Ask for help; talk it through."

- *Learning tactic*. Learn from others.

Two Related Models

While the *thinking* and *feeling* descriptors are the same as those in the popular Myers-Briggs type indicator (Myers, 1980), they are used in a very different context. The Myers-Briggs is a personality instrument that stresses differentiation, while the LTM focuses on learning options and problem analysis while stressing integration. The ways intuitives and sensors gather data—and the differences between what thinkers and feelers do with that data—are, however, directly related to the process of learning.

In another model, Kolb (1984) outlines a cycle of experiential learning beginning with "concrete experience," moving through "reflective observation" (a stage of reflecting on that experience) to "abstract conceptualization" (relating the process to existing meaning structures), and finally into "active experimentation" (a stage of action). Kolb's experiential learning cycle is just that: a cycle that learners go through in a sequential order. The LTM, like Kolb's learning cycle, stresses the importance of multiple options for understanding and processing information. It does not suggest a preferred sequence, however, or advocate using all learning tactics for all problems. The categories within the models are also different. For example, "accessing others" in the LTM is much more inclusive and active than "reflective observation" in Kolb's experiential learning cycle.

Both the Myers-Briggs Type Indicator and Kolb's experiential learning cycle are powerful models that are somewhat related to, but different from, the LTM. When seeking to improve leadership effectiveness and organizational productivity, the primary purpose of a model is to distill reality and help working managers develop a common language and frame of reference. No one model, therefore, is better than another. The proof of a model is how it helps individuals and organizations make sense out of their environment. For the manager seeking a broader repertoire of models, Kolb's experiential learning cycle and the Myers-Briggs Type Indicator are two models that are definitely worth studying.

Learning Tactics in Action: Tales of the Eye, Ear, and Foot

There are hazards in overreliance on a single learning tactic. Effective learners are aware of their bias toward one-dimensional learning and find ways to break the pattern. Table 9.1 lays out the problems implicit in each approach to learning. The diagonal—where the same approach appears in both row and column heads—gives the basic strategy for each approach; the "without" in the column head points out the hazards of one-dimensional learning.

The ear, eye, and foot examples in this section are condensed and paraphrased versions of the stories of three learners.

Hearing the Voice

A middle manager who managed a data processing center in a small town on behalf of a large financial services organization phrased his newly discovered insight in auditory terms:

"They closed another site and sent the work up here. I could handle that, but they wouldn't let me add enough people to take care of the increased workload. I was ready to reorganize, cut out a level of management, start a third shift, and bring in more temporary workers. I had it all laid out, and it was a good plan. But then, before I implemented it, I heard this small voice whispering to me, 'you're doing it to yourself again!' I was about to solo again—jump into action without talking to anyone—getting outside input. Looking back, I learned a lot by talking to my supervisors and the other processing site managers who had gone through workload increases and hiring freezes at the same time."

Seeing the Options

An executive director of a nonprofit service organization visualized alternative learning tactics:

"He [an employee] lied to me. As far as I was concerned that was it. I was mad and ready to do something about it. I had his termination papers processed. But they just sat there in my desk drawer, something kept me from pulling them out and giving him his walking orders. Finally, I sat down and wrote it out, using some of that journaling training I hated. I saw an old pattern emerge—making decisions based on my feelings is not always the best practice and

Table 9.1. Hazards of Limited Learning Tactics.

	ACTION without	THINKING without	FEELING without	ACCESSING without
ACTION	Engage the task: just do it!	Procrastination	Paralyzed	Talk it to death
THINKING	May not have the vital information. May not extract all the learning from the consequences of action. May repeat actions not successful in the past.	Gather data; work alone; think it through the past and the future	Overrespond to emotional aspects without the calming influence of reason/past successes	Lose the information that resides within formal sources or within one's self. Misuse others to avoid the task
FEELING	Ignore/deny feelings and slip into habitual responses	Intellectualize, rationalize to avoid the task	Acknowledge and manage tackling the unknown and uncertain outcome, the untested	Misuse others to avoid the task
ACCESSING	Reinventing the wheel, no support, may offend	Miss the learnings and support of others. Won't have the benefit of others to push, challenge your thinking	Unnecessary isolation	Seek out others for advice, support, information, coaching

Source: Dalton, 1995. Used by permission.

he had hurt my feelings. I thought about it, listed out the pluses and the minuses of firing him. Then I talked it over with the head of my board and she convinced me that I should give him another chance. Writing it out gave me a way to see the whole picture."

Moving the Feet

A middle manager who spent over a year agonizing over whether he should leave an unsatisfactory job and return to school finally took the right steps:

"I must have made fifty lists of the ups and downs of leaving. I really wanted to get out of there, but I was in an analysis loop. The more I analyzed the more unsure I became, and the more I needed to do more analysis. One day, I just threw away all my lists and got on with it—trusted my intuition and quit. It was the best decision I've ever made. Sometimes I have to follow the advice of that ad and 'just do it!' That's not easy for me, but I think I learned something."

Learning to Learn: Developing Better Hearing, Sharper Vision, and Fleeter Feet

Internalizing and using different learning tactics is a good-news–bad-news proposition. The good news is that better-balanced and more situational learning is the essential competence for new-glue leadership; it can facilitate individual relevance and organizational survival. The bad news is that it isn't easy; it is an against-the-grain struggle. It's not only our own grain we are moving against, it's the grain of other people's expectations and stereotyping. In the stressful world of the new reality, developing a more balanced and planful learning repertoire is not always welcomed by others. To move from entrenched, overwhelmed, and BS response patterns, we have to fundamentally change, and that change is often seen as threatening to those left behind. Kerry Bunker (personal communication, 1995) articulates it as follows: "The ability to learn is the new core competency and there is a conspiracy that is keeping it from happening. The two major players in this great conspiracy are (1) you, and (2) everyone else!"

Three things are needed to break out of Bunker's great conspiracy: an awareness that there are other, more appropriate, learning tactics; the courage to experiment with these new tactics; and support, reinforcement, and developmental feedback from others. It is a classic example of the unfreezing, moving, and refreezing process outlined by Lewin (Marraw, 1969). The unfreezing is the realization that old one-dimensional learning strategies aren't adequate to the new reality, and we need to explore other more relevant options. Moving involves both acquiring a cognitive map of new learning tactics and following the map, applying new and broader learning methods. Refreezing requires success with new learning tactics and reinforcement, affirmation, and support from others.

As is the case with the elusive quest for the big tool described in Chapter One, there is no single, foolproof technique that will lead to the acquisition of a wider range of learning tactics. Equifinality prevails; there are many ways to get there. A number of techniques and strategies were suggested in those previous chapters dealing with individual and organizational R-types. What follows are some additional ideas and approaches that will facilitate the development of the requisite ears, eyes, and feet.

Discover the Patterns in Your Learning History

Find out how you learn and how you developed your learning patterns. It is the necessary first step to becoming intentional in your learning tactics. Here are some suggestions:

•   *Seek out mirrors and have the courage to name what you see.* Performance appraisals, truth tellers, and formal and informal feedback will help you see yourself. Look for learning patterns. Ask others how they experience your learning and problem-solving orientation. Review the response types and use the worksheets to discover your type and your developmental needs. Write a description of your R-type and your self-assessment of your preferred learning tactics.

• *Map and explore your grain.* Learning grain, the predisposition toward certain learning tactics, is formed by personality, motivational drives, and early developmental experiences. There are many useful and readily available instruments that help provide insight to personality and motivational style. They all have a slightly different twist. Don't take them as the gospel or as the big tool, but only as one data point in your quest for insight.

An interesting grain-mapping exercise involves writing and explaining the learning implications of our early commandments. These are messages that we have received in childhood that have helped shape our current grain. Bunker (1994b) provides the following examples:

Early Commandments—Parental Quotes to Live By

- Work hard if you want to amount to anything.
- Anything worth doing is worth doing well.
- You can learn more by listening.
- If you can't say anything nice . . .
- I suppose if she jumped off a bridge, you would too.
- Silence is golden.
- If you want it done right, do it yourself.

• *Map and explore your current learning tactics.* Find your primary learning tactic on Figure 9.1. Next find the one you use least. List your second and third preferences. You should now have a ranking of your learning preferences. Think of a recent event requiring learning or complex problem solving. Reflect on how you approached it. Did you use more than one learning tactic? What was the sequence? Would starting with a different set of tactics or exploring more options have resulted in a different outcome?

Commit to Multiple Learning Tactics

The first step in the road to becoming a more relevant learner is the decision to go against the grain and take personal responsibility for expanding your learning options. This requires the realization that there is a fair probability that the range of learning tactics that got you where you are won't keep you there or help your organization prosper. There are two ways you can reinforce your decision:

• *Build a human support system.* High-performance athletic teams and even high-performing athletes in individual sports do better with a coach—someone to give them advice, feedback, and support. Going against the grain and developing new learning tactics can be frightening and overwhelming without a support system. Support systems can be individual learning partners, small-group learning networks, professional associations, and occasionally—provided they are of the learning variety—entire organizations. The purpose of a support system is honest feedback, help, and above all, support and encouragement.

• *Keep a learning journal.* There is great power in writing out your thoughts, frustrations, and progress. The process of journaling not only forces reflection, it also provides a way to review and measure your progress. The key is to do it regularly and honestly. There is no best format, but it is important to keep the journal focused on the problem, the context, and your learning tactics.

Seek Work That Provides a Developmental Stretch

Challenging work in a variety of contexts is the best arena within which to try new learning tactics. The pain isn't worth the gain if new learning tactics are applied to easy or already understood problems. Lazy learning is really no learning and there is no developmental payoff for the individual or productivity gain for the organization.

• *If you seek leadership development, honor the equation:* $V + C + A = LD$. The most significant leadership development happens on the job (McCall, Lombardo, and Morrison, 1988). There are, however, some requisite conditions that are spelled out by the formula $V + C + A = LD$ (Moxley, 1995). V stands for variety of assignments; C stands for challenging assignments; and A is for the ability to learn from the assignments. The end result is LD, or leadership development. All three elements need to be present in this, the basic developmental equation. It does no good to work on the ability to learn and on alternative learning tactics without applying those tactics to a diversity of challenging assignments.

The Painful Promise of Gagging

Going against the grain—*gagging*, to make the initials into a short and evocative word—is an unnatural act. It is, however, an act that is a precursor to relevancy in the new reality. Figure 9.2 represents the four-stage process of a successful gag.

Figure 9.2. Anatomy of a Learning Experience.

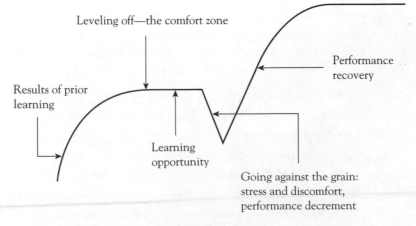

Source: Adapted from Bunker and Webb, 1992, p. 5.

- *Stage One*. The first stage involves the harvesting of prior learning. It is characterized by a performance improvement curve. This upward performance curve can measure something as individual as the compensatory improvement involved in better management of a bad golf swing (as was the case with George in Chapter Three); it could be something as corporate as U.S. automobile manufacturers reaping profits by manufacturing large, fuel-eating cars of mediocre quality; or it could be something as mutual as a marriage that flourishes during the honeymoon stage.

- *Stage Two*. In the second stage, performance levels off and begins to decline. This leveling off is followed by a wake-up call, which is often transmitted in the form of a crisis. The golfer plays more difficult courses against better competition, and as he becomes more chronologically gifted, he is physically less able to compensate for bad swing fundamentals. His performance level then drops. The wake-up call of global competition and changed buyer demands quickly deflates the arrogance and nearly sinks the U.S. automobile industry. The basic needs for autonomy and individual achievement create a crossroads in the growth of a relationship.

- *Stage Three*. After the wake-up call comes the choice stage: sink or swim, learn or decline. The golfer can choose to accept the discomfort and ego deflation of a decrement in performance while learning the correct swing mechanics. The U.S. automobile manufacturers could either accept declining market share and profits or decide to move against the grain—drop their arrogance and learn to make better cars, listen to the market, and accept the reality of global competition. The marriage partners have the option of accepting superficiality, separating, or choosing to redefine the boundaries of independence and mutuality.

This stage involves choice. The gagging choice is not as easy or as apparent as it might seem to someone analyzing the process and external to the action. The reluctance to let go of something that is dysfunctional but predictable is all too familiar to those accustomed to the dynamics of abusive relationships. Old tapes, early commandments, and the need to look good and seem competent are very powerful. Bunker's great conspiracy is operant; the two forces who collude to stop you from making the learning choice are you—and everyone else!

• *Stage Four.* Performance recovers as the new learning takes hold, and this stage often involves a spurt of steep growth. Having learned the correct swing, the golfer moves beyond his best compensatory performance; the automobile industry gains market share and creates much greater value for both their customers and their shareholders; the marriage achieves a balance of intimacy and autonomy that allows it to be far more productive than in earlier stages.

Little Engines, High Hopes, and Self-Efficacy

Figure 9.3 depicts the cost of choosing not to learn, avoiding a learning experience. The lost learning equates to lost performance—and in the new reality, avoiding the learning choice at best dooms individuals and organizations to the land of the entrenched, and can often lead to overwhelmed and BS responses. In a time when everything is changing all the time, avoiding the learning response is not a wise choice. For both the individual and the organization, this is a case where the pain is definitely worth the gain.

The little blue engine pulling all those cars filled with toys and good food up the mountain engaged in what motivational psychologists now call positive self-talk. "I think I can—I think I can—I think I can," the engine puffed to itself as it willed its way up the slope (Piper, 1930, p. 33). Some children's books contain profound truths and convey them with an unpretentious clarity that is in stark contrast with the sometimes stilted language of the behavioral scientist, who would describe the little engine in terms of self-efficacy, or as exhibiting a behavioral manifestation of expectancy theory. However you say it, that engine had a compelling vision of making it up that mountain. It had, as Sinatra sang, "high hopes,

Figure 9.3. Anatomy of a Lost Learning Experience.

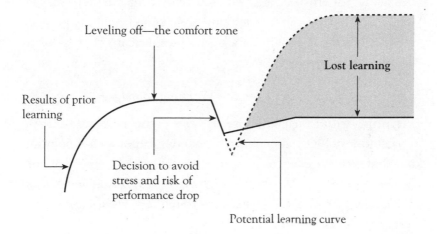

high, apple pie in the sky hopes." Whatever you call it, high hopes, positive expectations, or self-efficacy; the "I think I can" approach that helped that little engine make it up that impossible slope helps those choosing the learning option move against the grain.

Self-Efficacy: The Gag Lubricant

It comes down to one fundamental truth: learners go against the grain; nonlearners don't. This is manifested at both the individual and organizational levels. Individuals who want to be relevant to the new reality make the learning choice; organizations that want to ensure their survival choose the path of collective learning. The learning choice triggers the gag response, and one way to make that response go smoother is by using the lubricant of self-efficacy and the "I think I can" psychology.

As was discussed in Chapter Five, the primary learning response pattern involves engaging and growing. This is a positive and optimistic response. The learner has enough self-esteem to take a risk. The learning response is the opposite of the primary overwhelmed response, which is withdrawing and avoiding (Chapter Two); a behavioral pattern associated with low self-esteem. Self-esteem, positive expectations, self-efficacy, and positive self-fulfilling prophecies are among the many labels for the lubricant that helps to facilitate the learning choice.

Ten Practical Lubricants for the Working Manager

Beginning with Douglas McGregor's classic theory X and theory Y expectations (1960), there have been a number of writers pointing out that positive expectations are directly linked to positive outcomes (for example, Vroom, 1964; Lawler, 1973; Bennis and Nanus, 1985; Eden, 1992). Here are ten ways to relate positive expectations to the facilitation of gagging.

• *Give more strokes than lashes*. Self-esteem and positive expectations are built by affirming people's self-worth, telling them how good they are, praising them, and reminding them that they can be even better. I have followed managers around for a day and counted both the number of affirming and encouraging comments they made and the number of times they were critical or blaming. Most of us seriously underestimate the number of negative and blaming comments we make and overestimate the amount of affirmation we project. This can be tested. Find someone to shadow you for a day. If you are anything like most managers, you will be surprised even though you know someone is keeping track. One problem is that many managers feel they are being phony or insincere by passing out positive comments all day. My experience is that that is incorrect, you almost can't overdo it. You need at least a ten-to-one ratio of strokes to lashes. Catch your fellow workers, not just those who report to you, doing something right and tell them! You don't build self-esteem in a survivor workforce by assuming people know when they are doing something well and only telling them what they are doing wrong. Practice this on yourself as well, engage in positive self-talk. If you are not positive about yourself, you will not be able to do much for others.

- *Reward and recognize learning and ignore nonlearning.* It is a basic tenet of behavioral conditioning that you reward desired behavior and ignore nondesired behavior. When you suspect someone is gagging, offer encouragement, support, and recognition. Remember that what seems natural for a learner goes against the grain for the other R-types. When in doubt, recognize and reward. Unless nonlearning behavior is destructive, it is better to ignore it than to recognize it. In the stress-filled world of the new reality, any attention, even for the wrong behavior, is often perceived as better than no attention.

- *Engage in expectation and self-efficacy training.* This has two dimensions: helping managers develop the skills to coach and facilitate positive expectations, and working with employee groups to increase their self-efficacy. Although not widespread, this type of training is emerging as a very practical tool (Eden, 1992). Level-three interventions designed to break organizational codependency are the essence of self-efficacy training (see Appendix A).

- *Go off campus to rebuild self-esteem.* Volunteer or other outside organizations provide safe environments for personal revalidation and ego rebuilding. Working in these external settings is a very good way to rekindle high hopes, which can be transported back into the workplace and used as a gagging lubricant. Brockner (1995, p. 39) writes, "If survivors take action to reaffirm their self-integrity, they will be less adversely affected by factors that have the potential to threaten their sense of self. Moreover, the steps taken to reaffirm self-integrity do not have to be in the same arena that threatened self-integrity in the first place." Brockner's idea is based on the self-functioning theory of Steele (1988), and offers an option to managers wishing to rebuild self-esteem in a safe place.

- *Be a cheerleader.* Although it may not fit the controlled, laid-back, conservative cultural norms of many organizations, there is great lubricating power in the manager who is public, positive, and unrestrained in his praise of learning behavior. Most managers over-intellectualize and underemotionalize.

- *Be a salesperson.* Overwhelmed and entrenched employees need to be sold on their inherent potential. The manager is asking these employees to take a big risk and experience the frustration and anxiety of gagging. It's essential to sell them on their own potential and remind them they really can do it. I have seen some incredibly effective managers do nothing but sell people on their own inherent value and ability. In organizations populated by entrenched and overwhelmed employees, management is in the business of selling affirmation and hope.

- *Dance the Pygmalion two-step.* The Pygmalion effect is defined by Eden (1992, p. 271) as "a type of self-fulfilling prophecy . . . in which raising manager expectations regarding subordinate performance boosts subordinate performance. Managers who are led to expect more of their subordinates lead them to greater achievement." The Pygmalion two-step is a dance of expectations. The first step is to expect that others around you have high expectations for themselves and the organization. The reciprocal step is to have these expectations of yourself. It is a very powerful mutual dance that won't stop unless someone's expectations drop.

- *Give equal time to the body, mind, and spirit.* Self-esteem is not built solely through cognition. You can do a lot through introspection, but you can't analyze your way to high hopes. We tell people to feel good about themselves, not think good about themselves. Although thinking may lead to feeling, managers need to externalize more. Smiles, cheerfulness, celebrations, humor, and body language that emphasizes openness and acceptance are external manifestations of positive feelings. These behaviors are contagious and lead to the rekindling of human spirit, which in turn stimulates the learning response. Self-esteem is also rebuilt through taking care of ourselves physically. Weight gain, drug and alcohol abuse, lack of sleep, overwork, and lack of exercise are all legacies of the overwhelmed and the entrenched response patterns. Managers need to model healthy lifestyles. They will help themselves and stimulate others.

- *Create organizational myths and stories that reinforce the learning choice.* This is a two-step process. The first task is to change organizational myths and stories that promote negative expectations. That little engine would not have reached the top of the mountain if it had puffed out, "I know I can't—no one ever has—my boss tells stories about all the engines that couldn't!"

The second step is to develop stories and myths that celebrate learning and promote positive expectations. This is a very important role for top managers. Eden (1992, p. 299) writes, "The impact of myths on expectations can be particularly insidious and persistent because, as part of the organization's culture, myths summarize complex, underlying beliefs and assumptions. . . . Therefore it is the job of the CEO and other top leaders with high visibility and credibility to change organizational culture and replace pernicious myths with positive ones."

- *Lighten up!* Attempting to manage and lead organizations filled with overwhelmed and entrenched employees is a daunting task. Working to instill positive expectations, staying "up" and optimistic, and helping others move against their grain and become better learners is emotionally and physically draining. You can't be all things to all people. It's a balancing act. You need to care enough to put your spirit into your work, but you can't take it so seriously that you damage either your spirit or your health. There are two realities. The first is that it really is only a job and if you lose it you can, and believe it or not, you will, find something else to do. The second reality is that they may miss you, but not for very long! We all overestimate our importance and indispensability to organizations. Take care of yourself and do the best you can. After all, it really is only a job!

Angling Lessons: Perspective and Observations

Past measures of human intelligence have focused on analytical and verbal ability. At least in postindustrial Western society, the ability to analyze and manipulate complex spacial and quantitative relationships and the verbal skills to communicate in linguistic abstractions have been the defining factors of intelligence. It is not coincidental that the value of these abilities paralleled the industrial and information revolutions.

There is an increasing awareness of a new cluster of abilities called "emotional intelligence" (Goleman, 1995). Emotional intelligence is not really new, it has just been in the closet for a long time. Those with a high emotional intelligence quotient are able to authentically connect with their own and others' emotions and maintain and establish empathetic relationships. They are able to use their intuition and feelings to deal with others, make decisions, and solve problems. Emotional intelligence is the stuff of the new glue and it is not by chance that it is making its debut concurrent with the dawning of the new paradigm. In today's survivor workforce, level-two and level-three interventions, facilitating grieving, and breaking organizational codependence are accomplished through emotional intelligence (see Appendix A).

If the old intelligence was about analytical and verbal ability, and the new emotional variety is about empathy and intuition, the future intelligence will be about learning. This LQ or learning quotient employs both the verbal and analytical IQ of the past and the emotional abilities of the new EQ. The learning competencies outlined in this chapter are a blend of the analytical and the emotional. The ability to map and understand our learning tactics is an analytical process; the courage to go against the grain and experiment with a broader repertoire of learning options requires emotional intelligence. From a managerial perspective, both can be stimulated by the creation of an environment of hope and positive expectations.

10

Breaking Free

In her sensuously husky voice, singer Janis Joplin articulates a basic tenet of existential philosophy: "freedom's just another word for nothing left to lose." The existential philosopher Jean Paul Sartre phrases it differently, stating that we are "condemned" to be free (Sahakian 1971, p. 354). It is, indeed, our fate, whether we perceive it as condemnation or opportunity, to live through the advent of the new reality, and, at one level of analysis, both individuals and organizations appear to have lost a great deal. Employees have lost job security and the sense of long-term organizational identity. Organizations have lost the predictability of managing a dependent and internally oriented workforce.

There is, however, a very different way of looking at these so-called losses and our existential condemnation. There is a classic joke that defines a pessimist as one who sees a glass filled to the midway point with water as half empty, while an optimist sees it as half full. There has been a recent twist to the joke that adds a third perspective, that of the reengineering expert, who sees the glass as too big! A fourth way of looking at this picture is that the depth of the water or the size of the glass are not the main points. What is at issue is the purpose of the water, how it can be used to serve others, and the congruence of the process with the human spirit of the server.

There is incredible power in our condemnation, and the flip side of our losses is that we have lightened our existential load; we no longer have to define who we are in terms of where we work. Freedom may, indeed, "be another word for nothing left to lose," but there is a great deal to gain. An outgrowth of our condemnation to the new reality is that we can choose to be free from the stifling constraints of a one-down, dependency relationship with our organizations. We can break the bonds of organizational codependency and choose the path of freedom. The power of this choice is that we can invest ourselves in the satisfaction of meaningful work, serve others, reclaim our self-esteem, and pursue the learner's path. The organizational payoff is immense: a workforce filled with free, independent employees working on tasks congruent with their human spirit—resulting in long-term sustainable competitive advantage.

The Yin-Yang Freedom Dance

Breaking free, making the learner's choice, is not a one-time event, it is a lifelong struggle. It is an against-the-grain experience requiring courage and new ways of thinking for both individuals and organizations. The employee must choose to break free and claim the new freedom and the organization must accommodate and facilitate that choice. This mutual pursuit of the learning way requires a holistic connection between the individual and the organization not unlike the yin and the yang of Eastern philosophy. In a yin-yang relationship, both halves are incomplete and need each other to achieve the unified whole. The mutual interaction between individual and organization is the dance of freedom and learning: it is the Yin-Yang freedom dance. What follows are five aspects of that dance, with the individual taking the yin part and the organization the yang.

- *Yin One: Don't put all your emotional or psychological eggs in the organizational basket.* First of all, it's a bad bargain; you can't trust that the organization will hold onto the basket. Baskets have been dropped in the past and will hit the ground again. At a deeper level, making your self-esteem and sense of relevance contingent on remaining employed by one organization reduces your freedom and sets you up to be a victim.

• *Yang One: Don't provide baskets.* Engaging in a strategy that sets up long-term dependency relationships with employees is expensive and limits organizational flexibility. Dependent employees are motivated by pleasing, fitting in, and, most of all by staying employed. They are not the independent, customer-focused risk takers you need to thrive and compete in the new reality.

• *Yin Two: Focus externally, serve the customer—not your boss or your career.* By serving customers, you'll help yourself and your organization. Pleasing the boss and playing organizational politics in service of your career is an unhealthy artifact of the old reality. Being clear about who your customer is and spending your time providing value-added service is a much less energy draining and more personally affirming use of your time than wallowing in the internal ambiguity of a dying bureaucracy.

• *Yang Two: Insist on an external focus; don't ask for abstract, long-term corporate loyalty.* Your organization will be best served by insisting that all employees have a clear customer, and have a very concrete understanding of their value-added. Fuzzy notions of corporate loyalty, expectations that employees spend time and energy fitting in through impressing the boss, making internal presentations designed to please top management, or rigidly adhering to internally oriented corporate rituals and dress codes—all this wastes time, diffuses energy, and gets in the way of doing meaningful work in the service of others.

• *Yin Three: Equate who you are to what you do, not where you work.* Who you are should not be where you work. Your sense of identity, self-esteem, and purpose should not be contingent on your organizational affiliation. When you allow your identity to reside in your workplace, you become organizationally codependent. In the new reality, this puts you in a permanent victim relationship, perpetually one-down with your organization. Connect your self-esteem with your profession, with the work you do, not with where you happen to be doing it. That way when you leave you can bring two things along: your skills—and your self-esteem.

• *Yang Three: Don't foster dependency relationships*. Benefits, pay systems, status symbols, and policies that favor tenure over performance and internal pleasing over customer service are nonfunctional artifacts of the old reality. If organizational praise and rewards are contingent on anything other than doing quality work in the service of others, the system is toxic to long-term organizational survival. Independent and task-focused employees who look outward toward their customers are the way to ensure a robust future.

• *Yin Four: Accept and embrace the fact that you are a temp*. Even though we all don't work for temporary help firms, we are all temporary employees. This is a liberating revelation to many of us. We no longer have to play political games and attempt to outwit the bureaucracy. We are eventually going to lose our jobs anyway and are free to put our energy and invest our identity in our work and our profession.

• *Yang Four: Stop giving employees mixed messages: own up to the new employment contract*. Many organizations are conflicted and confused about the psychological employment contract and employees often hear very different stories from the top and from first-line management. It is very difficult for long-tenured employees, who are often in upper-middle management and top management, to drop their old-paradigm assumptions concerning motivation, commitment, and loyalty. To admit that the new psychological contract is short term and task focused as opposed to long term and career focused is to say what got them to where they are is no longer valid, and since many are organizationally codependent, such an admission diminishes their sense of relevance. Organizations need to work hard to get clarity and acceptance of the new psychological contract. Autonomous employees who are free from the internal constraints of the old bureaucracy are a source of competitive advantage and organizations need to cultivate and nurture that freedom.

- *Yin Five: Find work that is nutritious.* The first ingredient of the new glue is human spirit, and applied human spirit is the currency of the realm in the new reality. There is power, excitement, and amazing productivity when our work is congruent with our personal mission and values. This work is nutritious to our human spirit. We have all experienced times when we were lost in our work, when it turned us on and when time seemed to stand still. We can't achieve nirvana every day, but we can find the kind of work and the kind of culture where we can move closer to connecting our human spirit with our work.

- *Yang Five: Don't create a toxic culture or allow work that does not nurture the human spirit.* Human spirit is a powerful, fragile, and elusive commodity. It is impossible to quantify and it can't be contained in job descriptions or organization charts. All employees at all levels in all jobs come to organizations with incredible human potential. We have human potential because we are not robots to be acted upon, to be reengineered. We are adventurers sharing a common bond—our brief journey together through human existence. If organizations can provide the spark that ignites our reservoir of human spirit and allow us to apply it to work that we perceive as meaningful, they have unleashed a powerful competitive weapon of creative energy. Cultures that are toxic to the kindling of this human spirit are those that exert too much control and pigeonhole people into narrow roles and jobs. Nontoxic cultures are flexible, developmentally optimistic, and very creative in matching work to individual.

The Good, the Bad, and the Ugly

There is amazing power in choice. We simply do things better when we have the choice of not doing them. Volunteer armies generally perform better than those made up of conscripts. The best relationships between spouses or significant others are those where each party has the option of leaving and chooses to stay in the relationship. Couples who stay together despite the free, open, no-fault option of leaving form a much more meaningful and productive bond. Conversely, couples who stay together for no reason other than their fear of leaving foster resentment, victimization, and often abuse.

In the new reality, the worst reason to stay with an organization is the fear of leaving. This motivation provides a one-way ticket to the land of the entrenched and overwhelmed for both individuals and organizational systems. Organizations that will thrive in the new reality are those that will be filled with employees who have the option to leave, but choose to stay because of the work. Those that will fail will be populated by employees who are only there because they are afraid to go elsewhere. Successful organizations of the new reality will have a great deal in common with the best volunteer organizations. This is demonstrated in the following stories of the good and the bad, and their ugly comparison.

The Good!

The first time I walked through the front door of the Human Service Alliance (HSA), I asked the person at the reception desk to tell me the number of full-time employees in the organization.

"We are all volunteers here," he said with a smile. "Even though I'm on the board, as you can see, today I'm a volunteer receptionist. There are no employees at HSA."

"How can you run a complex organization like this with only volunteers? Who sets priorities, handles conflict, keeps the place on track?" I asked.

His response captured what I now believe to be the essence of organizational productivity and survival in the new reality. "We leave our personal agendas at the door and our work here is measured in terms of whether or not it helps our guests, not whether or not it helps us!"

Many years of working with organizations and recent experience in the all-too-common petty and territorial world of volunteer and nonprofit organizations triggered a warning voice deep within me. "Sure they do! Believe that when you see it," it whispered to me!

I now have seen it and I do believe it. HSA does four things: cares for people who are dying, takes care of severely developmentally disabled children so their parents can have a day off, provides diagnosis and treatment for people with chronic pain, and offers a mediation and dispute resolution service.

Whether bathing the terminally ill, preparing food, cutting the grass, fixing broken water pipes, or doing the accounting, all the work is done by volunteers in a spirit of service, and the level of that service is outstanding! It is, as described in the title of a recent book about this organization, *Better Than Money Can Buy* (Kilpatrick and Danzinger, 1996). The quality of the volunteer work done at the HSA, twenty-four-hour care for the dying and the disabled, is an example of the power of applying human spirit to the service of others.

The HSA organization is not a cult. Most volunteers have other jobs and other lives. They encompass a wide spectrum of education and background—business executives, laborers, consultants, secretaries, physicians, law enforcement officers, and lawyers. Although they all leave their personal agendas on the doorstep on the way in, many of them retrieve them on the way out.

The Bad!

The organization I shall call Lakeside Technologies rode the high-tech wave of the late sixties and the seventies. It was founded by an entrepreneurial engineer, who wisely surrounded himself with a group of aggressive MBAs. Through a combination of proprietary technology, government contracts, and the luck of hitting a niche market at the right time, Lakeside experienced phenomenal growth.

As time progressed, the market grew competitive, the technology grew obsolete, and the government contracts shrank. The founder and his MBA Mafia grew wealthy through stock options and withdrew from day-to-day operations, and the organization was led by a committee of externally hired executives who had nothing in common except their greed and territoriality.

I passed through Lakeside's front door just after the beginning of what was to become a very steep decline in people and profits. They were in the midst of their first major across-the-board reduction and my client, the human resources vice president, wanted a program to turn the organization's morale around. He wanted it completed in two months, the end of that quarter, because that was when he told the CEO he'd have it done and that was when his budget ran out.

"It's mission impossible," I said. "You're not going to fix the kind of problems you have in this organization with a program and you're not going to do it in two months!"

I then gave him my analysis of Lakeside's issues, which can be summarized as follows:

• The workforce, at least the people I surveyed in the headquarters complex, approached their work as though it was a sentence. In the manner of prisoners checking off dates on a calendar, they counted the days and hours until their next vacation, holiday, or even the weekend. They stayed in the organization not because they chose to be there, but because they were afraid to leave. They were locked in by above-market pay and benefits, and self-perceptions of nontransferable skills. The majority of the workforce exhibited R-entrenched behavior patterns with an increasing migration to the land of the overwhelmed.

• They definitely didn't need another program. They already had too many; the organization had overdosed on programs! Almost all of them were internally focused and supported by multimedia communications that resembled an external advertising campaign. These programs were immensely time consuming, requiring endless meetings, reports, and presentations to upper management. The organization had so many of these programs and the employees spent so much time tending to their administration and bureaucracy that the programs were construed as the basic work of the organization by a significant portion of the employee population. These internal programs were in danger of clogging Lakeside's arteries and there was imminent danger of a complete blockage.

- No one, including the top managers I met, had a clear take on their market, their strategies, or their customer. The entire organization seemed consumed with internal reports, committees, status symbols, and career management. The problem was there were no real careers to manage, most employees were either going out the door or hanging on by the skin of their teeth, and all the internally focused activity represented entrenched behavior that was counterproductive in the new reality. What Lakeside badly needed was a sense of purpose and an external orientation.

The Ugly!

The Human Service Alliance and Lakeside Technologies represent polar extremes on a continuum. The ugly reality, however, is that the vast majority of organizations—profit or nonprofit, volunteer or paid—are much closer to Lakeside than to HSA. A comparison between the two illustrates organizational characteristics that stimulate freedom and productivity, and those that cause codependence and victimhood.

Characteristics of Freedom-Oriented Organizations

Those organizations with characteristics that are closer to the HSA end of the continuum are framed as *freedom oriented*.

- *People in freedom-oriented organizations are there because they choose to be, not because they have to be.*

The power of HSA is in the volunteer nature of the workforce. People come there because they can apply their human spirit and their passion to their work. They feel empowered, fulfilled, and committed.

The weakness of Lakeside is that people are there because they are afraid to leave and are connected to the organization by pay, benefit, and status systems that are all external to the most powerful connector: their passion and human spirit. They feel bought, trapped, and victimized.

- *The first priority of people in freedom-oriented organizations is to help others; self-help follows.*

The work in HSA is grounded in service to others, not promotion of self. The paradox of letting go of self-centeredness and moving to other-centeredness is that both grow, but you have to start with the other. It is an old principle, one I call escaping into good work. If you feel bad about yourself, find people who feel worse and help them. There are two very positive results: you feel better and so do they!

The work in Lakeside is grounded in internal political bickering and self-promotion. The individual nature of incentive compensation and departmental territoriality are two manifestations of a zero-sum game mentality. Helping others is perceived as weakness and taking away from self. This results in a narrowness and a sense of organizational despair.

- *People in freedom-oriented organizations are very clear on their customer, their product, and their value-added.*

HSA volunteers know exactly who they are trying to help and what they need to do to facilitate that help. Sometimes it involves direct interaction with the customer, as in personally caring for a terminally ill guest. Sometimes it is indirect, such as preparing a meal, cutting the grass, mopping the floor, or spending a wet, cold weekend in a crawl space fixing a broken water pipe (Kilpatrick and Danzinger, 1996, pp. 43–44). Regardless of the degree of directness, at HSA all the workers are clear about how what they do benefits the ultimate customer. That clarity, along with a culture that values all tasks equally, promotes the pride and the quality of service that characterizes a freedom-oriented organization.

Many of the employees at Lakeside have a fuzzy understanding of how what they do serves a customer. This is particularly true in the middle-management ranks, whose members spend nearly all their time in internally oriented task forces and committees, or preparing for presentations intended to impress other internal people. Without a clear connection between their tasks and customer needs, employees find no relevance in their work. With no externally validated meaning, they find no pride or self-esteem in their work.

- *People in freedom-oriented organizations have a galvanizing societal purpose.*

Organizations are a means to an end. Organizational survival is not an end in itself. This societal purpose is very clear in HSA. The organization is a vehicle to serve society by alleviating chronic pain, helping families through a death experience, and granting parents of developmentally disabled children a respite from their grinding responsibilities. This purpose is what pulls people into the organization and causes them to help perpetuate it.

Commercial organizations also have a societal purpose. They provide jobs, pay taxes, and provide products and services that are valued by others. Making money is like breathing, organizations need to make a profit to stay alive, but all successful organizations have a broader purpose than simply making money. Automobile companies meet peoples' needs for transportation, banks help people manage and invest their money, and Lakeside provides technical solutions to a number of human problems. The societal purpose of Lakeside, however, is not articulated, understood, or internalized by the employees. It is difficult for them to harness their spirit to a purpose as vague and impersonal as providing value to the shareholders. People need a more personal and galvanizing purpose.

- *People in freedom-oriented organizations have unifying structures and processes.*

HSA volunteers are not just turned loose. There are procedures and checklists for everything from returning a call to cleaning the yogurt machine. Freedom needs some structure or it will degenerate into anarchy. The trick is to align the level and the nature of the structure with the purpose of the organization. HSA has done a brilliant job with this alignment. The procedures are clear but not heavy, and there is a well-used methodology for volunteer input and procedural revision.

Lakeside has a bewildering array of confusing and overlapping policies and procedures for almost everything. They have too many rules and no one seems clear as to either their purpose or the process for their revision. Because of the internal orientation and the resultant need for self-validation, they have a many-layered hierarchical structure with several approvals necessary for both routine and exceptional transactions. They need fewer policies, fewer levels, and a basic alignment of their structure and procedures with their purpose.

- *People in freedom-oriented organizations consciously work to eliminate victim mentality and to work and learn in groups.*

HSA has internal training programs on "letting go of victim mentality," and in "the fundamentals of group work" (Kilpatrick and Danzinger, 1996, pp. 73, 97). The ability to take personal responsibility for feelings and actions along with the skills to work in groups or teams are central to the learning response. HSA has developed a culture that facilitates the development of these new-reality behaviors.

Lakeside employees work in an interlocking web of victimhood. It pervades all levels and all functions. Although there are some groups attempting to work together, they appear to lack the skills and values to truly function. To survive and compete in the new reality, Lakeside needs a major systemwide intervention to break organizational codependency and to develop into a group-oriented learning organization.

Mad Max and Cool Carl

In order to directly embrace a freedom-oriented environment, it is necessary to drop perspectives that have worked in the past but are no longer relevant in the new reality. This change of worldview is illustrated by the differing perspectives of Mad Max and Cool Carl.

Mad Max

Those of us who have worked in the government, served in the military, or worked in old-paradigm organizations have been conditioned and influenced by the philosophy of the pioneer German sociologist, Max Weber. The name may not be familiar, and we may not recognize the extent to which we have been influenced, but Mad Max (throughout his career he suffered from what many now characterize as a bipolar disorder), has definitely had an influence on us. He is the father of classical bureaucracy, and whether we admit it or not, we have been living under the guidance of his progeny throughout our tenure in old-reality organizations.

Mad Max's creation has taken a bad rap. In many ways, it was the ideal organizing principle for the old reality. It gave us job descriptions, merit pay, role-based performance appraisal, formal succession planning, objective application of rules and procedures, and separation of the office from the officer. Max had good intentions: he was attempting to make administration more rational and less subject to the personality of the charismatic leader (Kasler, 1988, p. 167). Under Mad Max's bureaucracy, promotions and pay would be based on merit rather than birthright. (Weber's frame of reference was turn-of-the-century Germany.) The way he proposed protecting organizations from the eccentricities of aristocratic leaders was to wring every ounce of humanity from the system. Mad Max would not get wealthy on today's speaking circuit with the theme of the following quotation, but it nonetheless was his central message:

"Bureaucracy develops the more perfectly the more it is 'dehumanized,' the more completely it succeeds in eliminating from official business, love, hatred, and all purely personal, irrational, and emotional elements which escape calculation" (Parkin, 1982, p. 35).

The struggle for freedom and relevance in the new reality involves letting go of past assumptions of the way people are, and the way things ought to be in organizations. It has been my experience, however, that when even the most committed learners look deeply enough into the mirror they will see the shadow of Mad Max staring back at them. The traditions of classic bureaucracy run deep in our culture. Our democratic heritage causes us to be wary of strong leaders and build systems to immunize ourselves from the influence and potential arbitrariness of any one individual. That's exactly what Mad Max had in mind. To check out your level of closet bureaucratic discipleship, consider your reaction to the following: "The fully developed bureaucratic apparatus compares with other organizations exactly as does the machine with the nonmechanical modes of production. Precision, speed, unambiguity, knowledge of files, continuity, discretion, unity, strict subordination, reduction of friction and of material and personal costs—these are raised to the optimum point in the strictly bureaucratic administration" (Parkin, 1982, p. 34).

Cool Carl

Although Carl Rogers was trained as a classical psychodynamic therapist and began his career by practicing for twelve years in a Rochester, New York, social agency, he is most noted for his contributions to the so-called human potential movement. He had a unique ability to keep his cool in therapy sessions. A transcript of one session indicates that there were silences of up to fourteen minutes. He writes about this session, "I believe that a word count would show that the client uttered little more than 50 words in the first of these interviews" (Meador and Rogers, 1979, p. 166).

Cool Carl believed in giving others unconditional positive regard, responding to them with empathy, and approaching an interaction with a fellow human being with genuineness (Rogers, 1961). That's it! Rogers believed if you could do those three things people would learn, grow, and develop. To Cool Carl, people were endowed with a natural actualizing process that unfolded on its own if others didn't block it. If others got in the way, however, as in being conditional in their regard, the process got stuck and the individual needed help.

Breaking free involves making the choice of dropping out of the predictable and increasingly dysfunctional world of Mad Max, moving forward, taking the risk of relevance, and traveling the path of learning with Cool Carl. This transition is not easy. It involves losing some comforting elements of the past and embarking upon the exciting but uncertain quest for future significance and meaning. This passage involves two steps: saying farewell to Max, and greeting Carl.

The Path of Relevance: Losses and Opportunities

Moving out of Max's world is not an easy relocation. We often have second thoughts and the impulse to turn around. The rewards, however, are definitely worth the discomfort. We need to push forward.

Step One: Goodby Max!

The first step on the way to freedom and relevance involves letting go of the safe and predictable comfort of the old reality. Bureaucracy offered structure, form, predictability, and protection. It fit the culture of the old reality; contrary to the emotion conjured up by the word, Max's creation worked well. Although the time has come to say farewell to Mad Max, the parting is not easy and cannot happen without experiencing a sense of loss. There are three primary categories of this loss:

- *Loss of certainty.* The system articulated by Mad Max was nothing if not certain, predictable, and clear. There were paths for decisions, concrete job descriptions, and clarity of individual roles and responsibilities. We were protected by the objectification and quantification of our jobs. We could do long-term career planning within one organization. Although classic bureaucracy never lived up to Max's expectations, and we now know it is an oxymoron to speak of dehumanizing human systems, it nonetheless—for all its faults—provided a much more certain and predictable system than those in the new reality.

- *Loss of institutional security.* In Max's bureaucracy, we made a bargain—we gave an organization our loyalty and trust and it gave us security. Although this old employment contract has been widely violated and has led to layoff survivor sickness in many organizations, a large number of employees have still not done the necessary grieving. To move forward, the loss of the past must be experienced at an emotional level, and there is no loss that is as necessary to work through as the erosion of the old employment contract. In our bureaucratic past, we lived by fitting into and accepting the protection of the structure. In the new reality, we live by our wits, our skills, our service to customers, and our ability to market ourselves.

- *Loss of internal community.* The old, bureaucratic world provided a predictable internal community that remained relatively stable over time. Many employees moved through entire careers with the same colleagues. They were able to establish long-term friendships and develop primary reference groups within their organizations that often spanned many generations. Although there are small-group and work-team affiliations in the new reality, they are much more temporary and task focused. The loss of a stable intra-organizational network is another casualty of the paradigm shift.

Step Two: Hello Carl!

The inexorable unfolding of the new reality has given us a choice. We can retreat to the world of the entrenched, succumb to victimhood and withdraw to the residence of the overwhelmed, or choose the learning path and advance into the unchartered yet exhilarating waters of the free. The Rogerian way is the ambiguous choice of freedom and learning.

- *The opportunity for self-discovery.* Cool Carl was not only cool in his relationship with others, he was cool with himself. Self-understanding is a necessary precondition to helping others. According to Rogers, the person forming a helping relationship had to be strong enough not to lose individuality, secure enough to truly accept the feelings and perceptions of others, and developmentally optimistic enough to see the other person as "becoming" (Rogers 1961, pp. 50–56). These traits require self-discovery and are essential for those who would pursue the learning path.

• *The opportunity to help others.* Freedom leads to service. If we do not serve, we cannot be truly free—we become oppressed by our own selfishness. True freedom carries with it the responsibility of helping others to break free. The learner is not only working to help increase the productivity of an organization in the abstract, but personally helping to move entrenched employees, stop the slide of the overwhelmed, and bring self-awareness to the BSers. Those taking the learning path are missionaries of optimism. Rogers was developmentally optimistic to his bones. There is no room for cynicism in the world of Cool Carl.

• *The opportunity to be relevant.* The decision to become a learner, a helper, and to accept the uncertainty of freedom is to make the choice of relevance. To choose to remain in the camp of Mad Max is to make the choice of obsolescence, and that choice leads to victimhood, counterproductivity, and ultimately to a wasted work life. The world of Cool Carl is a place of service and relevance. It is a place where there is the possibility of connecting your human spirit to your work and, in doing so, to the service of others.

Breaking Free: Perspective and Observations

For individuals, breaking free involves reclaiming and taking personal responsibility for our self-esteem and connecting it with what we do and not where we work. For organizations, it calls for letting go of the false comfort of Mad Max's bureaucracy and building organizational systems around collective learning. It involves developing cultures where people come to work because they choose to be there, not because they have to be there. These transitions are not easy: they involve going against the grain of many years of individual conditioning and organizational stereotyping. Here are three final thoughts for facilitating that transition.

Start Where You "R"

You can get there from here! R-factor analysis provides a map that not only helps assess your own and your organization's current status, but also outlines practical suggestions as to how to move forward. Chapters Six and Seven structure a framework for analysis, and Chapters Two through Five offer specific examples and guidelines. A plan can facilitate change, and it certainly restores a sense of control for both individuals and organizations experiencing fundamental transition. R-factor analysis provides a framework for this planning.

Pursue the Protean Way

The Greek god Proteus had the ability to change form in response to adversity, yet still remain a god of the sea. Although you can't be all things to all people, you can be more things to more people, including yourself, and still not lose your basic identity. This is the profound learning of the Protean way and is good news for those individuals and organizations who are locked into intractable, nonproductive response patterns for fear of losing their fundamental values or purpose. Robert Lifton, a psychiatrist who has devoted much of his professional life to understanding survivors, writes in *The Protean Self* (1993, p. 82), "A survivor, fundamentally, has two psychological possibilities: to shut down or to open out." The Protean promise is that in opening out, letting go of outdated and nonproductive response patterns, we are still able to hold on to our essence.

Begin with the Heart

Breaking free is an inside-out process. It does not happen to us, we make it happen for ourselves, and the primary tool is not our head, it is our heart and our human spirit. We can't analyze ourselves into making a spiritual choice. Breaking free, for both the individual and the organization, is a matter of faith and hope. The propellant for the individual breaking organizational codependence and reclaiming self-esteem is not the head, it is the heart. The organization that makes the choice to learn in the collective and to discover ways to connect peoples' human spirit to their work is making a spiritual, not a rational, choice. In the new reality, human spirit is not soft and irrelevant. It is the incredibly powerful propellant that allows us to take the risk of relevance.

Appendix A

A Frame of Reference

This appendix provides a brief review of five concepts discussed in *Breaking Free:* layoff survivor sickness, organizational code-pendence, the old and new realities, and the four-level intervention model. For a more in-depth treatment, readers are referred to my previous book, *Healing the Wounds: Overcoming the Trauma of Lay-offs and Revitalizing Downsized Organizations* (1993).

Layoff Survivor Sickness

The dynamics of layoff survivor sickness are illustrated by what happened to Arnold, who works in what in the United States is sometimes called a Baby Bell—a regional phone company created during the breakup of the nationwide monopoly. His father spent his entire career in the Bell System, thus making Arnold an official "Bell Brat." Until divestiture, Arnold's life was a carbon copy of his father's: a secure job, lots of friends, regular salary increases, and, in the predictable future, a good retirement plan.

Then the bottom dropped out! First came divestiture, then a series of confusing organizational changes, and finally, wave after wave of layoffs. Arnold saw his friends and coworkers lose their jobs. He wasn't sure he would survive. He felt violated, vulnerable, angry, and fearful. The rules had changed. Up until then, he assumed that as long as he was loyal to the organization, was honest, and met performance standards, he could count on his job. Throughout his career, he'd been told and told he was a long-term asset to the organization; suddenly he felt like a target, a cost to be reduced. His productivity dropped; his risk taking ceased; he grew moody and depressed. Arnold developed a classic case of layoff survivor sickness!

I have discovered a worldwide epidemic of this survivor sickness. It exists in boardrooms and on shop floors. I have found it among German middle managers, in Canadian government officials, U.S. technical professionals, and British bankers. It exists in all areas, across line and staff functions, in nearly all organizations.

Characteristics of Layoff Survivor Sickness

There are four general characteristics of this widespread organizational ailment:

- The root cause, as is the case with other classic survivor symptoms, is a deep sense of violation.

- The symptoms include four clusters of feelings: fear, insecurity, and uncertainty; frustration, resentment, and anger; sadness, depression, and guilt; and unfairness, betrayal, and distrust.

- Organizational survivors cope in ways that are neither personally healthy nor organizationally productive. The two primary coping mechanisms involve an aversion to risk taking and reduced productivity. Thus organizations with survivor workforces are attempting to meet global competition by fielding workforces of wounded survivors who won't take risks and who suffer from impaired productivity.

- The symptoms, without intervention, do not go away and often seem to intensify over time.

The good news is that I have found that survivor sickness can be cured, and the resulting wake-up call frees up energy and the ability to tap into undiscovered depths of creativity and productivity for both individual and organization. The bad news is that the cure requires changing patterns of leadership and work behavior that are deeply embedded in organizational cultures and individual expectations. Throwing off the shackles of layoff survivor sickness requires breaking out of a codependent relationship—and that requires both courage and faith on the part of the individual and the organization.

Organizational Codependence

The term *codependence* was first used to describe the unhealthy relationship of a spouse or significant other to an alcoholic (Beattie, 1987). The codependent partner enjoys a positive self-image only when the alcoholic other stays dry. The codependent's self-esteem is contingent on someone else's addiction. The concept of codependence has now been expanded to gain insight into a wide variety of situations caused by the unhealthy practice of defining oneself through the actions and behaviors of others. A female therapist told me the story—I think it is a joke that makes a point—of a woman who had nearly drowned. She was saved in the nick of time and dragged to the beach. After her lungs were pumped out, her rescuer asked, "What did you think about as you approached death?" She replied, "My husband's whole life flashed through my mind!"

We do not want to make our self-esteem or sense of relevance contingent on the behavior of any individual or organization. It is not good for us or for them; it limits and diminishes both parties. The language and theory of codependence provides a clear lens for visualizing the unhealthy dependence that is the underlying cause of layoff survivor sickness. To the extent that we index our self-esteem to remaining employed with a single organization, we are organizationally codependent. What follows are five observations in regard to organizational codependence.

Organizational Codependence: Five Observations

- The conscious fostering of organizational codependence has been a cornerstone of the past fifty years of human resource strategy. Organizations have had benefit plans, status symbols, group purchasing plans, social clubs, compensation systems, promotional patterns, and many more implicit and explicit policies and cultural norms that have fostered tying employees into organizations. These systems have worked very well and a large number of employees have become dependent on their organizational affiliation for much more than a paycheck.

- Organizations have done such a good job in fostering a dependency relationship at the emotional and social level that many employees react to a threat to their employment security with a pervasive sense of violation. A question implied throughout this book is, "If who you are is where you work, what's at threat if your job is at threat?" This is at the heart of the matter. What is at stake if you are organizationally codependent in the new reality is your self-esteem and sense of meaning.

- The way to develop an immunity to organizational codependence is to refuse to put all your social and emotional eggs into the organizational basket. Define yourself by your work, not where you do that work. Don't put a taproot into the organization for your self-esteem; develop a diffuse root system into family, community, profession, and place of spiritual nourishment.

- Many organizational leaders who were raised under the old reality have difficulty letting go of three basic management tenets grounded in a codependent strategy: they equate dependence with commitment, motivation with loyalty, and paternalism with leadership.

- Organizational codependency is systemically reinforced by organizational norms and myths carried over from the old reality.

Employees are not only conditioned into a codependent relationship by their employer, but by powerful outside institutions such as
family and schools. It requires an act of courage on the part of the
individual and faith on the part of the organizational system to
break codependency and form a new, more productive relationship.

Old and New Realities

I use several terms interchangeably, hoping to create a linkage with
those who don't connect with one set of labels. I know that some
people become hooked by the word paradigm, yet, to others, it
depicts the basic change in worldview that Kuhn (1980) meant
when he resurrected it from obscurity. Similarly, I have found that
some people put a too-literal interpretation on the increasingly well-
accepted terms, "the new employment contract" and "the old
employment contract." These and other labels are words, struggling
to communicate a basic—and I believe fundamental—change in
the connection of person to organization. I call this change the old
and the new reality.

The Old Reality

The old reality, the old psychological contract, or the old paradigm
are labels for a pattern of beliefs that held that a person who main-
tained proper performance and compliance with the organizational
culture could count on remaining employed with one organization
until voluntary departure or retirement. The reciprocal organizational belief was that loyalty required the individual's total commitment. The organizational response to this commitment and
dependence was an acceptance of the obligation to provide a lifetime career.

The New Reality

In the new paradigm or the new psychological contract, there is no
long-term job security. Part of this new reality is that we are all

temporary employees. One way of looking at it is that employees are short-term costs to be managed and often reduced; as opposed to long-term assets to be developed over a career. Organizations have no obligation to plan lifetime careers for all employees and employees have no obligation to blindly trust that their organizations will take care of them.

Three Observations on the Old and New Realities

The Change Is Irrevocable. You can't turn back the clock. Programs geared to getting back to normal will not work. What is taking place is a fundamental redefinition of the relationship of employee to organization. Efforts to tell employees that "if you just make these cuts" or "just get with the new program," (quality, reengineering, customer alignment, and others), "we will finally get through it and things will get back to the way they were," communicate the wrong thing. The nature of the change is that despite the most well-intentioned, well-designed, and badly needed improvement programs, things will never get back to normal!

Many Leaders Still Don't Get It. In his retirement speech to Congress, General Douglas MacArthur gave fame to the refrain from a military ballad, "Old soldiers never die, they just fade away" (Prochnow and Prochnow, 1979, p. 122). It has been my experience that, too often, old-paradigm leaders don't die—and they take way too long to fade away! In prolonging the agony, they send mixed messages and often cause harm to the long-term future of their organizations. Despite well over a decade of turbulence and irrefutable evidence of the advent of the new reality, a surprising number of well-intentioned and well-educated organizational leaders are attempting to manage their organizations as though the paradigm shift is simply a temporary irritant. This is often reflected in what I call the bait and switch vision.

The Bait and Switch Vision. Leadership literature is filled with definitions of the leader as a person who generates a galvanizing vision:

one that aligns an organization's resources toward a compelling future state. There is certainly nothing wrong with a powerful shared vision. No organization can long move in one direction through today's turbulent and ambiguous environment without the steady guidance of a compelling vision. The problem comes when organizational leaders use the power of a new galvanizing vision to take people to an old past, which, despite its familiarity and comfort, cannot be recreated. What follows is an abridged and paraphrased version of a speech given by a sixty-year-old top executive of a Midwest electronics firm to the semiannual meeting of the organization's top sixty managers:

> We've got a lot of work to do and it's not going to be easy. We need to be more customer driven, create a total quality environment, pay attention to our costs, and commit ourselves to a limited number of products that will give us sustained competitive advantage. This is a lot of change, but in the end it will be worth it. We can renew our employees' faith in leadership, regain their commitment and long-term loyalty, and most importantly, restore their employment security. If we stay focused on our vision we can get past today's problems and return this organization to the culture and values that made it great in the first place.

This speech has a means-and-end problem. The means were appropriate: this organization needed to be market focused with higher quality and reduced costs if it hoped to survive. The end, however, a return to guaranteed long-term employment in response to employee loyalty, was a fantasy that couldn't happen. Unfortunately, I hear many speeches and see many vision statements designed by organizational leaders who came up under the old reality and have great difficulty accepting that the old psychological contract and the related dependency-based assumptions of management and motivation are no longer relevant. These bait and switch visions are, all too often, accepted by a workforce that is also anxious for a "return to the future." The outcome of this collusion around a vision that can never be achieved is a deepening sense of employee violation and further erosion of top-management credibility.

Change Has No Built-In Benefit

The old reality was not necessarily bad; the new reality is not necessarily good. The old psychological contract grew out of the post–World War II era. We had the ability to mobilize large and—in the positive sense of Mad Max's much-maligned term—bureaucratic organizations. Big, paternalistic organizations grew and fit the needs of people to put down roots, purchase homes, and raise families. The old reality fit the times. It helped build an incredible array of products and innovations. It led, at least in most Western nations, to a standard of living that was previously unknown to all but the very wealthy.

The change to the new reality is part of a global, macro, socio-economic, and technological revolution. It is a no-fault process and there is no advantage in looking for someone to blame. We are well into a new, and very different relationship of person to work. Despite the predictions of futurists, none of us have any real experience with this new reality. All of our management models and motivational theories are rooted in the old reality and there is no certainty. I have, however, observed a few things and hypothesized some others. I have seen that often the customer is better served by new-reality organizations and that an increasing number of people are more whole and creative as a result of decoupling their self-esteem from their organizational security. There is still a great deal to learn. Asking people to be happy over the prospect of an ambiguous and uncertain future or to totally reject a system that has served us well for the past sixty years is not a productive exercise.

The Four-Level Intervention Model

The four-level intervention model pictured in Figure A.1 was developed to provide a frame of reference for taking action.

Figure A.1. Four-Level Intervention Model.

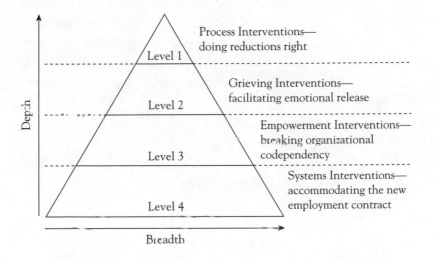

The levels are:

• *Process interventions*. Level-one interventions deal with the way layoffs take place: the process of doing layoffs. They do not provide a cure for survivors or help organizations develop systems that are in alignment with the new reality. They are, however, very important in that it is much easier to help the survivors with a good process.

• *Grieving interventions*. Level-two interventions are focused on helping survivors deal with their feelings and emotions and are critical to the catharsis necessary for letting go and moving forward.

• *Codependency-breaking interventions*. Level-three interventions (often individual acts of courage), involve recapturing individual self-esteem and disconnecting it from organizational membership.

• *Systems interventions*. These interventions are processes, policies, and organizational cultures that accommodate the new reality. They allow individuals the autonomy to put their spirit into their work, and free organizations to serve customers without becoming paralyzed by internal issues around status and control.

Although the four-level pyramid is a stage model, intended to convey the increasing depth and breadth of each successive intervention, what happens within organizations is always different from what academic models portray. I have found that level-one interventions sometimes lead directly to level-four systems changes, and that the act of breaking codependency (level three), can stimulate grieving (level two).

Another way I have found the model useful is with the time frame of the interventions, as shown in Figure A.2. With this perspective, levels one and two can be conceptualized as transitional interventions, and levels three and four can be seen as more long-term in nature.

Figure A.2. Broad Stages in the Revitalization Process.

TRANSITIONAL
INTERVENTIONS:

Working through the pain and stress of the immediate change and uncertainty. Laying the groundwork for revitalization.

LONG-TERM
INTERVENTIONS:

Breaking the cycle of blocked learning and organizational codependency. Fostering and nurturing healthier psychological linkages between employer and employee.

Summary

The concepts of survivor sickness, organizational codependence, the old and new realities, and the pyramid intervention model are the theoretical underpinnings of my revitalization work with individuals and organizations. I have found that they stand my ultimate test: they make sense to—and help—real people in real organizations.

Appendix B

R-Factor Genealogy

The current manifestation of the R-factor model is primarily the creation of Kerry Bunker. In parallel with Bunker's professional experience and orientation, the model has three roots.

The first root was a research effort that took place at AT&T from the late seventies to the mid-eighties and focused on management stress and coping. This study started before, and continued well into, the trauma experienced by that organization due to deregulation. Bunker contrasts the pre- and post-deregulation phases of the project when he says that he "started studying stress before they really even had any!" (Bunker, personal communication to the author, 1996).

The next root developed as a result of research at the Center for Creative Leadership during the late eighties and early nineties, which sought to understand successful managers' learning tactics. A central event in the development of the R-factor model was a one-year study of the ways that a group of high-potential managers learned how to learn (Bunker and Webb, 1992).

The third and still growing root involves the Center's current work in helping individuals and organizations cope with the effects of downsizing. What follows is a review of each of these three roots.

The AT&T Studies

AT&T has a well-deserved reputation as a place where the applied behavioral sciences have been used to better understand and facilitate management development. It pioneered the development and use of assessment center technology for a variety of organizational applications (Howard and Bray, 1988; Thornton and Byham, 1982). It also provided an environment that stimulated long-term human resources research. Bunker (1994a) describes the environment in 1977:

> The organization granted the group the freedom to design and conduct basic research with no direct responsibility for developing programs or otherwise applying its findings . . . the charge was elegantly simple: design and conduct major research projects that would ultimately contribute to the identification and development of capable managers and future corporate leaders [p. 60].

Within this fertile ground, a study of the relationship of leadership to ambiguity by Moses and Lyness (1988) led to an early quadrant model. Four distinct coping styles emerged from this project, which involved in-depth interviews with over forty executives. With one dimension as the "requisite skills to manage in ambiguous environments," and the other the "comfort level in ambiguous situations," four styles emerged: high comfort–high skills, called "adaptive"; high comfort–low skills, "unconcerned"; low comfort–high skills, "stylized"; and low comfort–low skills, "overwhelmed" (p. 330).

Bunker was involved in another study focusing on managerial stress and coping. This effort, conducted in four phases between 1978 and 1986, involved a sample of over two hundred male managers and a separate group of fifty female managers. Subjects experienced a variety of assessment processes including interviews, personality measures, projective tests, stress and coping indices, and defense mechanism inventories (p. 65). An initial analysis of the first three phases resulted in two very different profiles: "stress seekers" who tended to react to stress positively, and "stress avoiders" who reacted negatively (Bunker, 1983, pp. 9–10).

In a paper presented to the American Psychological Association (1983), "Ambiguity and Stress: Toward a Conceptual Linkage," Bunker connected his two-dimensional stress seeker–stress avoider concept to the four ambiguity coping styles developed by Moses and Lyness (1988). He writes:

> While the stress research results have been presented as a two-way coping breakdown, a careful examination of the profiles yields many parallels to the Lyness and Moses ambiguity coping model. . . . The objective of this section is to expand the Stress Seeker/Stress Avoider concept to fill the cells of the ambiguity quadrant model. While the components of this expansion represent hypothesized characteristics, the conceptualization is based upon the rich behavioral data of the stress project [pp. 10–12].

He then outlines four "hypothesized stress responses arrayed by ambiguity quadrants" (p. 13). These are: "adaptive," which contains many similar characteristics to the learning response; "stylized," which is somewhat similar to the entrenched response; "unconcerned," which relates to the BS response type; and "denying," which is analogous to the overwhelmed response type.

In another two-by-two matrix, Bunker (1994a, pp. 82–86) reports on phase three of the AT&T stress study by relating the dimensions of stress and adjustment. The four categories of this analysis are: low stress–low adjustment "whiners"; high stress–low adjustment "avoiders"; high stress–high adjustment "attackers"; and low stress–high adjustment "adaptors." In this analysis, the profile of the average "psychological symptom scores" for avoiders, attackers, and adaptors are computed and plotted against Bell System norms.

As can be seen, the R-factor model had its formative roots in the four coping styles of the ambiguity study (Moses and Lyness, 1988). These styles were then connected to the initial outcome of the managerial stress studies (Bunker, 1983), and, in turn, slightly renamed with three of the four styles measured and actually plotted against Bell System norms in phase three of the stress study (Bunker, 1994a). The next evolution of the R-factor model came at the Center for Creative Leadership, when learning tactics were factored into the equation.

The CCL Learning to Learn Study

The Center for Creative Leadership has had a long and abiding interest in studying the ways managers learn from experience (McCall, Lombardo, and Morrison, 1988). As a part of this effort, in 1989 the Center embarked on a one-year exploratory research project with a small group of high-potential managers (Bunker and Webb, 1992). One aspect of this project involved relating three coping styles from the AT&T stress study—avoiding, attacking, and adapting—to a four-part learning sequence: thinking, feeling, accessing others, and taking action. What follows are three insights from this analysis that facilitated the articulation of the R-factor model.

- *The avoider as a learner.* Avoiders are blocked learners who are ineffective in working their way through the learning sequence. They require help to get unstuck and apply more relevant learning tactics.

- *The attacker as a learner.* Attackers, although often successful problem solvers, tend to be prisoners of their

preferred mode of taking action. They get into trouble
by rejecting input from others and neglecting to formu-
late vision and strategy.

- *The adaptor as a learner.* Although they most often
  enter the learning sequence through thinking or
  accessing others, adaptors are equally adept and tend
  to access all of the learning tactics. They have learned
  how to learn.

The Center's learning to learn project made two contributions
to the evolution of the R-factor model. The first was that it served
as a vehicle for importing the AT&T stress study coping styles into
the research agenda of the Center. The second was that it directly
related three of those coping styles to the learning process.

CCL Leading Downsized Organizations Program

As a result of the publication of *Healing the Wounds* (Noer, 1993),
and the subsequent development of the Center for Creative Leadership's educational and research efforts, we have come in contact
with a wide cross section of individuals and organizations attempting to cope with the pain and trauma of downsizing. The R-factor
model has proven most helpful both in pointing out differential
responses to change and transition and in highlighting the centrality of the learning response to individual relevance and organizational survival. Recent developments (the past two years) include:

- A standardization of the descriptions and labels for the
  four quadrants. This has been the result of inputs from
  a variety of constituents as well as our own translation
  of previous manifestations of the model into the contemporary world of the new reality.

- Increasing use and acceptance of the model as a tool
  for helping individuals gain perspective on their own

and others' response to transitions in general, not just those associated with downsizing.

- Application of the model to organizations as well as individuals and, as outlined in Chapter Seven, use of the model to analyze individual and organizational fit.

Again, a word of perspective: the R-factor is not reality. It is only a model, and like all models it can help structure abstractions and communication patterns by providing a common language. Although the utility of the model is supported by a great deal of anecdotal evidence, it is, at this point in its evolution, an analytical tool; it does not purport to be a psychometrically sound assessment instrument.

Finally, the R-factor model is work in progress. We would welcome your ideas and comments.

References

Amabile, T. M., and Conti, R. "What Downsizing Does to Creativity." *Issues & Observations*, 1995, *15*(3), 1–6.

Argyris, C. *Intervention Theory and Method: A Behavioral Science View*. Reading, Mass.: Addison-Wesley, 1970.

Arnst, C., and Verity, J. W. "LOB, Anyone?" *Business Week*, Oct. 4, 1993, pp. 88–92.

Barrett, W. *The Illusion of Technique*. New York: Anchor Books, 1978.

Beattie, M. *Codependent No More: How to Stop Controlling Others and Start Caring for Yourself*. San Francisco: HarperCollins, 1987.

Bennis, W. G., and Nanus, B. *Leaders: The Strategies for Taking Charge*. New York: HarperCollins, 1985.

Bridges, W. *Transitions: Making Sense of Life's Changes*. Reading, Mass.: Addison-Wesley, 1980.

Brockner, J. "Self Processes in Leading Downsized (and Other Changed) Organizations." In D. Noer and K. Bunker (eds.), *Best Practices in Leading Downsized Organizations: Proceedings of a Conference*. Greensboro, N.C.: Center for Creative Leadership, 1995.

Bunker, B. B., and Alban, B. "Editors' Introduction: The Large Group Intervention—A New Social Innovation?" *Journal of Applied Behavioral Science*, 1992, *28*(4), 473–479.

Bunker, B. B., and Alban, B. *Large Group Interventions: Engaging the Whole System for Rapid Change*. San Francisco: Jossey-Bass, 1997.

Bunker, K. A. "Ambiguity and Stress: Toward a Conceptual Linkage." Unpublished paper presented at the annual meeting of the American Psychological Association, Anaheim, Calif., 1983.

Bunker, K. A. "Coping with Total Life Stress." In A. K. Korman and Associates, *Human Dilemmas in Work Organizations*. New York: Guilford Press, 1994a.

Bunker, K. A. "Early Commandments and Parental Quotes to Live By." Unpublished training aid. Greensboro, N.C.: Center for Creative Leadership, 1994b.

Bunker, K. A. *Ten Step Infallible Bell System Approach to Problem Solving.* Unpublished training aid. Greensboro, N.C.: Center for Creative Leadership, 1995.

Bunker, K. A., and Webb, A. D. *Learning How To Learn from Experience: Impact of Stress and Coping.* Technical Report #54. Greensboro, N.C.: Center for Creative Leadership, 1992.

Dalton, M. Unpublished training aid. Greensboro, N.C.: Center for Creative Leadership, 1995.

Dixon, N. *The Organizational Learning Cycle: How We Can Learn Collectively.* New York: McGraw-Hill, 1994.

Dixon, N. *Organizational Learning Competencies Survey.* Unpublished draft version 2.1, Interpretation booklet. George Washington University, Nov. 1995.

Donnan, S. "NAACP Board Chooses New President." *Greensboro News & Record,* Dec. 10, 1995, p. A1.

Drath, W. H., and Palus, C. J. *Making Common Sense: Leadership as Meaning Making in a Community of Practice.* Greensboro, N.C.: Center for Creative Leadership, 1993.

Eden, D. "Leadership and Expectations: Pygmalion Effects and Other Self-Fulfilling Prophesies in Organizations." *Leadership Quarterly,* 1992, 3(4), 271–305.

Emery, M., and Purser, R. F. *The Search Conference: A Comprehensive Guide to Theory and Practice.* San Francisco: Jossey-Bass, 1996.

Geisel, T. S. *Fox in Socks by Dr. Seuss.* New York: Beginner Books, 1965.

Goleman, D. *Emotional Intelligence.* New York: Bantam, 1995.

Hammer, M., and Champy, J. *Reengineering the Corporation.* New York: HarperCollins, 1993.

Harvey, J. B. "Encouraging Students to Cheat: One Thought on the Difference Between Teaching Ethics and Teaching Ethically." *Organizational Behavior Teaching Review,* 1984, IX(2), 1–11.

Hertzberg, F. "The Motivation-Hygiene Concept and Problems of Manpower." *Personnel Administration,* 1964, 27(1), 3–7.

Howard, A., and Bray, D. *Managerial Lives in Transition.* New York: Guilford Press, 1988.

Isaacs, W. "Dialogue." In P. Senge and others (eds.), *The Fifth Discipline Field Book.* New York: Doubleday, 1994.

Kasler, D. *Max Weber: An Introduction to His Life and Work*. Chicago: University of Chicago Press, 1988.

Katz, D., and Kahn, R. *The Social Psychology of Organizations*. New York: Wiley, 1966.

Kegan, R. *The Evolving Self*. Cambridge, Mass.: Harvard University Press, 1982.

Kilpatrick, J., and Danzinger, S. *Better Than Money Can Buy: The New Volunteers*. Winston-Salem, N.C.: Innersearch, 1996.

Kolb, D. *Experiential Learning: Experience as the Source of Learning and Development*. Englewood Cliffs, N.J.: Prentice Hall, 1984.

Kroeger, O., and Thuesen, J. *Type Talk: 16 Personality Types that Determine How We Live, Love and Work*. New York: Delta Books, 1988.

Kuhn, T. S. *The Structure of Scientific Revolutions*. (2nd ed.) Chicago: University of Chicago Press, 1980.

Lawler, F. E., III. *Motivation and Work in Organizations*. Monterey, Calif.: Brooks/Cole, 1973.

Lifton, R. J. *The Protean Self: Human Resilience in an Age of Fragmentation*. New York: Basic Books, 1993.

Marraw, A. *The Practical Theorists: The Life and Work of Kurt Lewin*. New York: Basic Books, 1969.

Maslow, A. H. *Motivation and Personality*. New York: HarperCollins, 1954.

McCall, M. W., Jr., Lombardo, M. M., and Morrison, A. M. *The Lessons of Experience*. San Francisco: New Lexington Press, 1988.

McGregor, D. *The Human Side of Enterprise*. New York: McGraw-Hill, 1960.

Meador, B., and Rogers, C. "Client/Person Centered Therapy." In R. J. Corsini (ed.), *Current Psychotherapies*. (2nd ed.) Itasca, Ill.: Peacock, 1979.

Merry, U., and Brown, G. *The Neurotic Behavior of Organizations*. Lake Worth, Fla.: Gardner Press, 1987.

Moses, J. L., and Lyness, K. "Individual and Organizational Responses to Ambiguity." In F. D. Schoorman and B. Schneider (eds.), *Facilitating Work Effectiveness*. San Francisco: New Lexington Press, 1988.

Moxley, R. Unpublished training aid. Greensboro, N.C.: Center for Creative Leadership, 1995.

Myers, I. B. *Gifts Differing*. Palo Alto, Calif.: Consulting Psychologists Press, 1980.

Noer, D. M. *Healing the Wounds: Overcoming the Trauma of Layoffs and Revitalizing Downsized Organizations*. San Francisco: Jossey-Bass, 1993.

Parkin, F. *Max Weber—Criticism and Interpretation*. Chichester, England: Horwood, 1982.

Piper, W. *The Little Engine That Could*. New York: Platt & Munk, 1930.

Prochnow, H. V., and Prochnow, J. V., Jr. *The Toastmaster's Treasure Chest*. New York: HarperCollins, 1979.

Rogers, C. *On Becoming a Person: A Therapist's View of Psychotherapy*. Boston, Mass.: Houghton Mifflin, 1961.

Ross, R. B. "Skillful Discussion." In P. Senge and others (eds.), *The Fifth Discipline Fieldbook*, New York: Doubleday, 1994.

Rost, J. C. *Leadership for the Twenty-First Century*. New York: Praeger, 1991.

Sahakian, W. S. *The History of Philosophy*. New York: HarperCollins, 1971.

Senge, P. *The Fifth Discipline: The Art and Practice of the Learning Organization*. New York: Doubleday, 1990.

Shepard, H. "Rules of Thumb for Change Agents." *OD Practitioner*, 1985, *17*(4), 1–5.

Steele, C. M. "The Psychology of Self-Affirmation: Sustaining the Integrity of the Self." In C. Berokowitz (ed.), *Advances in Experimental Social Psychology*. New York: Academic Press, 1988.

Thornton, G. C., and Byham, W. C. *Assessment Centers and Managerial Performance*. New York: Academic Press, 1982.

Tornow, W. W., and DeMeuse, K. P. "The Tie That Binds Has Become Very, Very Frayed." *Human Resources Planning Society*, 1990, *13*(3), 203–212.

Tripp, R. *The International Thesaurus of Quotations*. New York: Crowell, 1970.

Tuleja, T. *The New York Public Library Book of Popular Americana*. New York: New York Public Library, 1994.

Vaill, P. B. "Permanent White Water: The Realities, Myths, Paradoxes and Dilemmas of Managing Organizations." In P. B. Vaill, *Managing as a Performing Art: New Ideas for a World of Chaotic Change*. San Francisco: Jossey-Bass, 1989.

Vroom, V. H. *Work and Motivation*. New York: Wiley, 1964.

Weisbord, M. J. *Discovering Common Ground*. San Francisco: Berrett-Koehler, 1992.

Index

255